W9-BGN-490

THE MIGHTIER HUDSON

THE MIGHTIER HUDSON

The Spirited Revival of a
Treasured Landscape

ROGER D. STONE

ILLUSTRATIONS BY MICHAEL SLOAN

LYONS PRESS
Guilford, Connecticut
An imprint of Globe Pequot Press

To buy books in quantity for corporate use
or incentives, call **(800) 962–0973**
or e-mail **premiums@GlobePequot.com.**

Lyons Press is an imprint of Globe Pequot Press.

The author and the Sustainable Development Institute gratefully acknowledge the generous support of Furthermore: a program of the J. M. Kaplan Fund.

Text design: Sheryl P. Kober
Layout artist: Sue Murray
Project editor: Kristen Mellitt

Library of Congress Cataloging-in-Publication Data is available on file.

ISBN 978-0-7627-6395-5

Printed in the United States of America

10 9 8 7 6 5 4 3 2 1

For Flo

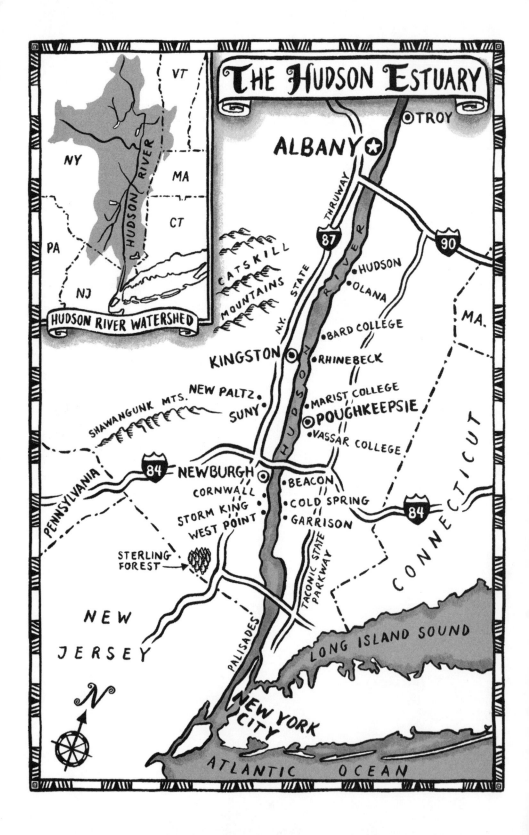

Table of Contents

PART I: GATHERING STEAM

CHAPTER I

The Walkway toward Redemption

LATE SPRING 2010. A PALE SUN SHINES WEAKLY ONTO THE HUDSON
River at Poughkeepsie. The *Clearwater*, a famous wooden sloop repli-
cating the sail-powered passenger and freight vessels that dominated
highly competitive river traffic before steamboats took over early in the
1900s, ghosts northward under a fitful westerly breeze. She is headed for
a weekend festival upriver. On the nearby Walkway Over the Hudson,
an old, abandoned railroad bridge reopened to pedestrians in October
2009 after a $38.8 million renovation, a diverse assortment of users is
out crossing the span. There are many dogs; children in strollers; babies
in backpacks and frontpacks; kids and grown-ups on Rollerblades; family clusters; many bikers, joggers, and hikers with walking sticks, some
sturdy, many overweight. There is a college student riding a unicycle; a
slender, heavily tattooed man sporting a Harley-Davidson undershirt;
a girl displaying her belly-button ring; an older woman in a long skirt,
blouse, and necklace; a young mom wearing a T-shirt making a simple
statement: WATER.

Along the way interpretive panels describe the steel bridge and its
history from 1889, when it opened as a link between Pennsylvania's
coalfields and New England's factories, to its demise by fire in 1974.
Signs also tell users of the "Talkway," a radio link to more information,
and spin the remarkable tale of how after the fire the bridge underwent

3

a Cinderella-like conversion from environmentally threatening eyesore into heavily visited scenic landmark. The 1.28-mile bridge is the world's longest pedestrian span, rising to the majestic height of 212 feet, gaining status as what the *New York Times* called "an unlikely ribbon of tranquility over the river that made New York New York." The scenic view up and down the river, of the partially restored Poughkeepsie waterfront on one flank and green Catskill foothills on the other, encourages inspiration. Says Beth, a Walkway worker: "It's amazing. When you get out there, everybody smiles."

How the Walkway became what it calls itself, a "linear park in the sky," is a remarkable tale. After the fire, the general assumption was that what remained of the bridge constituted a hazard and that its owner, Conrail, would be compelled to tear it down. But after a period of inaction, a temperamental Poughkeepsie handyman named Bill Sepe "became obsessed" with the pedestrian walkway idea, formed the nonprofit Walkway Over the Hudson organization in 1992, and set about to make it happen. In 1998 the group took over the ownership of the bridge.

In 2004 a new board with a broader vision staged a coup d'état to oust Sepe and assume the Walkway leadership. In 2007 this more sophisticated new team persuaded the community-minded Dyson Foundation to make an initial major commitment of $2.5 million to underwrite the engineering for the renovation. Once introduced to the idea, says Raymond Lamontagne, one of the foundation's board members, "This became something that Rob Dyson really aggressively wanted to do. He could envision the major positive impact the Walkway could make on tourism and on the regional economy, and he worked hard not only to provide the foundation's funding but also to get the public officials aboard and so on." As of mid-2011, the Dyson Foundation had committed a total of $15,958,000 to several different forms of support for the project, including payments made from 2006 to 2011 and ones scheduled through 2015.

Says Diana Gurieva, the foundation's executive director: "This was a stretch for us. But my board chair saw the potential of this project many years ago. He had the vision to see how marvelous it could be." Support also came from Albany, where state officials were in search of a highly visible way to highlight the four hundredth anniversary of Henry Hudson's much-celebrated 1609 cruise upriver. The 1909 tricentennial, featuring a million marching schoolchildren, a fifteen-hundred-vessel flotilla, and an astounding twenty-mile airplane flight by Wilbur Wright, was a hard act to follow.

With the Dyson commitment up front, and construction funding from several New York state coffers, the Walkway renovation took only sixteen months and opened to the public with great fanfare in October 2009. It had become a New York State Historic Park, with ownership transferred to Albany, and the original Walkway group transformed into a "friends" organization with programming and fund-raising responsibilities. The bridge was an immediate runaway hit, attracting some 750,000 users during the initial year—way above what was foreseen. Former Walkway chair Fred Schaeffer said he was "just astonished" by the turnout. "I thought that most people using the bridge would be the usual kinds of hikers and backpackers," says Gurieva. "But it's attracted people from every walk of life. It's sort of like a commons." Early on a nasty, windy Saturday morning during the spring of 2011, I returned for a second look. Even then, users were out in force.

According to the consulting firm Camoin Associates, a conservative estimate would peg direct spending from Walkway visitors at $14.6 million per year and total tax revenues at $1.3 million for local counties plus the state. The effects are especially visible along Poughkeepsie's shoreline, a busy place during the industrial era of the nineteenth and up to the mid-twentieth century that later experienced a sharp decline. At the terminus of the Walkway, old buildings are being recycled for use as cafes and stores to service the new traffic. It's still a pretty shabby-looking downtown, but this shift is in progress. Five years ago, Walkway reported, Mary Francese and her husband Peter bought a warehouse for their art business in Poughkeepsie near the Walkway terminus. They had a junkyard and a print shop for neighbors. Pedestrian traffic was "more like a pedestrian trickle." Now a "surge of walk-in customers has invigorated their business," according to the Walkway team, and cafes and other businesses are sprouting or expanding.

Recently, the Franceses sold the building to a developer who was planning a restaurant, a brewery, and office space. In the town of Highland, signage pointing to the parking area at the bridge's western end remains inadequate. But at a sparkling new Super 8 motel where I spent a night, and at the Vigneto Cafe in Highland's funky little downtown, I heard ample praise for Walkway's role as a magnet for tourists.

In Poughkeepsie Ned Sullivan, president of the prominent nonprofit Scenic Hudson organization, drove me to a riverside circular turnaround where schoolchildren were tending a small garden. "Over there, across the river, is Franny Reese State Park," said Sullivan, pointing westward. "It's named after the great lady who was Scenic Hudson's cofounder. That priceless riverfront land was destined for development, an eight-hundred-unit complex right in the viewshed from the Walkway and the Mid-Hudson Bridge. Now that land is protected, and the park spreads across 251 acres with links to the Walkway Loop Trail." And the view from the bridge is unblemished.

The Walkway is a classic example of what planners call "adaptive reuse." The *New York Times* called it "an amazing project" and "the latest example of the new kinds of infrastructure—for tourism and recreation—that are reshaping the Hudson Valley." The superbly renovated High Line snaking through Manhattan's Lower West Side, long a decaying elevated 1.5-mile rail spur, was headed for demolition before local advocates stepped in and, after endless struggles, arranged for it to become a park and a great public space. Quickly, after its first section opened in 2009, the High Line came to symbolize the esprit of its neighborhood with a new Whitney Museum taking shape under its shadows and real estate values perking up even in the tough times of recent years. "What housing crash?" asked the paper.

> *All around, construction is buzzing and the landscape is filling up with new buildings and warehouse conversions, funky and sleek condominiums, hotels, galleries, and public spaces designed by big-name architects like Frank Gehry, Jean Nouvel, Richard Meier and Annabelle Selldorf. And other projects once trapped in limbo by the mortgage and construction financing crises are moving ahead.*

If such dramatic change is not likely to happen so quickly along the long-neglected Poughkeepsie waterfront, Walkway similarly makes a bold, almost edgy statement that over the longer term bodes well for adjacent properties. The project has come to represent a new burst of energy and spirit. Crowed Robert Dyson, with perhaps a touch of hyperbole: "As much as the Golden Gate Bridge defines San Francisco, we believe this historically significant and visually stunning pedestrian walkway will some day define the Hudson River Valley." And if you don't have a grand old trans-Hudson railway bridge to work with, how about fixing up an abandoned, 940-foot trestle last used as a bungee jumping platform? The Wallkill Valley Land Trust in Ulster County and the Open Space Institute are making headway on a $1.1 million drive for funds to renovate the so-called Rosendale Trestle for hikers.

The 116-year-old span crosses Rondout Creek, a Hudson tributary. It needs new decking and railings. And with New York Governor Andrew Cuomo's proposal to tear down the five-mile Tappan Zee Bridge, connecting Westchester and Rockland Counties at the river's widest point, has come the fanciful idea of saving $50 million in demolition costs by fashioning yet another Walkway.

Along the short (315 mile-long) but pithy Hudson River, examples of this sort of transformation are, today, in encouragingly ample supply. So is evidence of a seedy or neglected past. A highly selective journey predominantly southward from the river's origin at the mile-high Lake Tear of the Clouds in the Adirondacks would yield a mixed harvest of images. First stop might be a striking whitewater stretch of the river bordered by a vertical cliff called Blue Ledges, frequented by paddlers and fishermen stalking native brook trout with dry flies. With the nontidal portion of the river gradually widening as you continue southward, you would encounter nondescript old port and factory towns called Fort Edward and Troy and then the state capital, Albany, sporting a series of tall buildings appearing, like Brasilia, to be starkly devoid of human occupation. Then the nearby dam at Troy marks the northern extremity of the tidal estuary, as you glide past rolling orchard country to sharply contrasting communities.

Newburgh, on the western shore, remains what Robert F. Kennedy Jr. and John Cronin called it in their 1997 book *The Riverkeepers*: "a mean, sick, nasty, fetid little city" with a high crime rate. Across the way, on the river's eastern shore, are towns that were well off in colonial times and remain so, with handsome houses sporting river views of great beauty, some, such as artist Frederic Church's castle, Olana, welcoming eager visitors. A busy clutch of colleges—Bard, Marist, Vassar, the State University of New York at New Paltz—enriches local communities and cultural tourists with a great diversity of offerings.

8

Now in the mid-Hudson, you have horsey, affluent Millbrook to the east and the stirring Catskills to the west, then a range called the Shawangunks, whose extensive trails, cliffs, and parkland attract swarms of hikers, rock climbers, and bicyclists. Passing through the Narrows at fabled Storm King Mountain and the US Military Academy at West Point, you enter a region where sprawl lurks but remains mostly under control. Striped bass, bluefish, and many other fish species that use the Narrows for spawning remain in ample supply around here, though persistent toxic pollution generates official warnings against eating the river's bounty too frequently and the storied shad is in what authorities call "serious trouble."

Below the Narrows the estuary widens to become Haverstraw Bay, a preferred spot for commercial fishermen. People swim from little beaches in Croton and other Lower Hudson towns, which enjoy splendid views of the George Washington Bridge and the lofty Palisades stretching thirty miles along the river's west bank. Manhattan boasts the new Hudson River Park, a stirring ribbon of blue and green stretching five miles southward from Fifty-Ninth Street in Midtown to Battery Park City near Ground Zero in the financial district.

Along the way down the river, one frequently encounters signals of redemption, the new spirit that characterizes the Walkway. A vivid example is to be found one hundred miles upriver, in and around the town of Hudson and its seventy-five hundred people. Long a busy port, Hudson thrived early in the 1800s, when whaling captains from Nantucket, Martha's Vineyard, and New Bedford moved in to get away from British Navy attacks and to build sturdy houses and ships. Later, supplementing farming, came an industrial upsurge built around the ready availability of raw materials needed to make cement—limestone and clay—and the convenience of the river as a transportation artery. Cement from the region helped build the base of the Statue of Liberty, the Brooklyn Bridge, and the Erie Canal.

But when the region's smokestack industries gave way to less costly competition from the US South and overseas, Hudson, among many of the river's once-proud ports, degenerated into environmental and economic disarray. Unemployment skyrocketed as shops and residences shut down along Warren Street, Hudson's main drag. In what became an endless cycle of boom and bust in the town, corruption, crime, drug traffic, and prostitution flourished. At one time modestly populated Hudson boasted fifty bars. Famously, Governor Thomas E. Dewey once sent into the brothels a squad of state troopers to clean things up. They snagged, among others, several local cops. Recently, you could still find a handsome Victorian or earlier fixer-upper house in Hudson, on a quiet street lined with old trees, for a hundred thousand dollars.

In the 1990s a company called St. Lawrence Cement (SLC), a subsidiary of the Canada-based, Swiss-owned Holcim Ltd, sought to make Hudson and the adjacent town of Greenport the focal points for a restoration of the traditional economy. The company would close down cement manufacturing operations elsewhere and build a huge, $353 million new plant on two thousand acres of land it owned in and near Greenport. Coal would fire the plant, whose dominant feature would be a 363-foot smokestack. A two-and-a-half-mile conveyor system would carry finished cement from the plant to an elaborate dock for transfer to giant barges, some as long as 754 feet. This fourteen-acre riverfront industrial area would dominate the town's shoreline and preclude the opportunity to develop recreational and other waterfront uses; the company's lawyers argued that the facility would "result in overall net benefits to the waterfront due to the revitalization of an historically industrial/commercial zone." Other economic benefits the company claimed included fifteen hundred construction jobs, appealing to many citizens in what had become a chronically depressed area, and at least $800,000 in local tax revenue.

Building this complex required permits from no fewer than seventeen agencies and the submission of exhaustively detailed documents, including a sixteen-hundred-page Draft Environmental Impact Statement (DEIS) that was subject to a public comment period. Some in the community, especially former cement workers, many of them black, saw the proposed plant as a reliable source of well-paying employment and sided with the company. Making cement had sent their kids to college. Support for SLC also came from some entrenched politicians, including longtime mayor, Richard Scalera, who had received campaign contributions from the company.

But a fast-growing coalition of mostly younger opponents took shape as well. Some thirty organizations participated, with leadership from Scenic Hudson and a new ad hoc community-based group called Friends of Hudson that was formed specifically to oppose SLC. Two strong volunteer leaders emerged: writer Sam Pratt and art and antiques dealer Peter Jung. Friends of Hudson grew to impressive dimensions, collecting fifteen thousand signatures opposing the plant, generating a membership of forty-one hundred individuals, and raising two million dollars to fight the company.

Opponents stressed the sheer size of the project, the harm it would do to attractive alternative economic development activities such as recreation, tourism, and real estate development; environmental and health issues relating to air pollution and noise; traffic; and impacts on wildlife. After the construction period the project would, they claimed, result in the addition of exactly one net job. In large measure those advancing these objections were not old-timers in the region but newcomers—many refugees or weekenders from New York City—who, starting in the 1980s, had begun investing in bargain properties, removing the boards from long-vacant buildings along Hudson's Warren Street, and accelerating the emergence of a new economy based on art and antiques dealerships, recreation, and cultural and recreational tourism. Hundreds of historical properties beckoned.

The film *2 Square Miles*, made in 2005 by local residents Sven Huseby and Barbara Ettinger, covers in absorbing detail the Friends of Hudson group's struggles and early failures both in the ballot box and later at a public meeting of the Common Council at which the stone-faced majority of its members duly sided with the company. But the ultimate control over the company's application lay not in local hands but rather, thanks to a federal law called the Coastal Zone Management Act, with the state's Department of State and its Coastal Management Program. On April 19, 2005, in a benchmark twenty-page letter to the company, Randy Daniels, then the Department of State's secretary, thumbed the proposal on the grounds that it was inconsistent with "the type of private investment and the kind of commercial development that has been unfolding in Hudson in the past twenty years." The project's massive size, Daniels added, would do grievous harm to the town's efforts to reconnect with the river via tourism and recreational activities. That same day, in a dramatic reversal achieved by opponents after years of knocking on doors, the Common Council also overwhelmingly said no to SLC. Victory for the opposition came despite its having been greatly outspent by the company in its massive effort to win public and political support for the venture.

Part of the reason for the outcome was that then New York State governor George Pataki, a Republican and also a fervent environmentalist, had loaded the dice. "If he hadn't greenlighted that decision, it never would have happened," says Friends of Hudson leader Peter Jung. But part of the reason, too, is that over time, those opponents managed to guide the debate past polarization and class warfare. Sure, they had to keep reiterating the specifics. But as Miriam D. Silverman reported in detail in her book *Stopping the Plant*, they also delved deeply into broader questions having to do with quality of life. "The opposition was making an active effort to go beyond saying 'no' to the plant to saying 'yes' to a new vision for the future of the Hudson Valley," Silverman reported. Sam Pratt says the turning point was reached "when each of us decided in our own minds that the community was worth fighting for."

So the battle was won, but how about the war? Long ago, spokespeople for SLC stressed the idea that the Hudson Valley's traditional industrial might was a stalwart part of its history. But many sources confirm that by the 1970s the old cement-based economy was in bad shape, with plant closings and cutbacks due to increasingly severe competition from abroad for market share in the United States. Hudson had become what businesswoman Nancy Gordon, in a *Poughkeepsie Journal* interview, called a "really desolate" place. But then in came galleries, boutiques, and mini manufacturing installations such as Gordon's, a small plant that produces electronic equipment. Travel writers from such magazines as *Town & Country* published glowing reports. As of 2010, reported Peter Jung, the town was doing just fine. "We had a six months' downturn last year, but now you can barely get in. The B and Bs are fully booked, the streets are busy, there are all sorts of innovative new things going on."

In Hudson recently, I dined well at a jam-packed white-tablecloth restaurant on Warren Street called Swoon, one of half a dozen good places to eat along the main drag. Steps to protect the environment, especially air quality, have become far more widely popular, a waterfront revitalization effort for small boaters is beginning to catch on, and everywhere there are signs of new energy based on new values.

Not that the hazards have vanished: As of summer 2011, though SLC had long since dropped its plan to build the cement plant, Holcim was once again on the warpath, petitioning to use the deepwater port it still owned as a facility for the storage and shipment aboard giant barges of limestone aggregate from nearby quarries the company still owned. The old Friends of Hudson organization, revived, was fighting the scheme, and Pratt and Jung had founded a new citizen group to oppose the venture on the grounds of inconsistency with local waterfront revitalization planning. Once again, an outcome favoring "consistency" was being foreseen.

A similar revival is under way in the town of Athens (pop. eighteen hundred), just across the river from Hudson. Once a whaling port, Athens later experienced a long decline. It ended only when outsiders very recently discovered its ample stock of affordable and sturdy eighteenth- and nineteenth-century houses facing the river or surrounded by mature foliage on pretty side streets. Chief among these is a large yellow mansion with spacious grounds, owned by New York City lawyer Ashton Hawkins and his co-proprietor, Johnnie Moore. The property, called Hawkemoor, sits prominently at the edge of town on a hillside overlooking the river. The house boasts high ceilings and eleven oversize fireplaces with towering mantels, a gracefully curving staircase connecting the first and second floors, original hardwood floors and window glass, and lovingly tended grounds and gardens. A cast iron cookpot sits on a hook in the fireplace of the once heavily used kitchen on the ground floor.

Down the street the grassy River Front Park serves as a gathering place. Short walks away are a relatively new marina for small powerboats and a launching area for kayaks and canoes that was spanking new in the summer of 2010. A bulletin board at the nearby River Side Café, which boasts an impressive array of handmade desserts, advertises musical events and other cultural offerings. The side streets, even during an enervating summer heat wave, were alive with the clatter and bustle of houses under renovation. "The whole place has remained relatively unchanged," says Hawkins. "We have an open waterfront on one side and farmland on the other. There's no sprawl around. There are quite a number of people who've moved in full-time, some of them from far away. Change has been gradual and really for the better."

A few miles down a bucolic two-lane road, in Catskill, is Cedar Grove, where painter Thomas Cole lived and worked from 1825 until his death in 1846 and where he executed his most famous work, including the famous Course of Empire series. Rescued by the Greene County Historical Society, the property was opened to the public in 2001, and renovation continues. Artist Frederic Church's Olana, with its splendid viewshed, is a mere twenty minutes away across the Rip Van Winkle Bridge. The Olana Partnership, stewards of Church's iconic Moorish-style residence in Hudson, asserts that the SLC decision was "ground-breaking in that it changed the terms of the debate—rather than providing a choice between development and view preservation, it recognized that the preservation of views is a crucial piece of another model of economic growth, one that capitalizes on thriving tourism and innovative, sustainable industry, rather than outmoded heavy industry." Closer to Athens are hiking and cross-country skiing trails and swimming holes on Catskill Creek featuring crystal waters and vertical cliffs. All this lightly touched area is easily accessible—and mercifully free of highway congestion—by Amtrak train from New York City to Hudson and then a quick hop across the river by boat or car.

Hawkins cannot suppress his enthusiasm about the region's potential. "Of course there's a little 'us versus them' about all this," he says, "but I think there's something in it for everybody. There's a lot of money to be made in real estate up here, especially with the new incentives that are being provided and the care we're taking of our landscapes." Hawkins and Moore themselves run a substantial little cottage industry featuring a happy-looking assortment of gardeners, caretakers, and craftspeople. A growing population of Internet-liberated former New Yorkers adds force to these sources of employment.

And another example, the current effort to restore the 1812 Plumb-Bronson House in Hudson, suggests something of how powerful this historical-houses restoration movement has become. Back in the late 1990s, reported the National Trust for Historic Preservation's *Preservation* magazine, Hudson store owner Timothy Dunleavy discovered what remained of the Plumb-Bronson House, a handsome and distinctive 1812 structure later renovated and enlarged by the well-known architect Alexander Jackson Davis with help from the ubiquitous Andrew Jackson Downing. This house too has a grand spiral staircase, many other indoor amenities, and sweeping views of the river and the Catskills.

But the site had become a dumping ground, and the house was slated for demolition. Dunleavy was "bowled over," but he had founded a nonprofit organization called Historic Hudson and managed to have it lease the property from its owner, New York State, get it declared a National Historic Landmark, and launch its renovation. Grants sufficient to stabilize the building came from New York State's Environmental Protection Fund and other state and private sources, and progress is being made toward a full-scale restoration. The project, said John Winthrop Aldrich, for many years the state's deputy commissioner for historic preservation, is "worth all the huge effort it will require." By pitching in on this fund-raising challenge, Historic Hudson is creating viable jobs by caring for a rickety old house that had been destined for the scrap heap.

As I made my way across the Walkway under brightening skies, the sloop *Clearwater* passed under the bridge under full sail, a stirring sight. To the southeast one could see parts of the rejuvenating Poughkeepsie waterfront. Metaphorically, I was glimpsing part of a broad and compelling shift to a new economy, a development surge that is becoming ever more visible along the Hudson. Even in the current shaky economy, there is little doubt that the valley is on a roll. Long-depressed towns in far worse condition than Hudson or Athens ever were (Peekskill, Beacon, even parts of tattered Newburgh) have turned the corner toward new economic and cultural vitality. World-class attractions of relatively recent vintage range from a magnificent outdoor sculpture park called the Storm King Art Center to a proliferation of art, theater, dance, and music offerings at Bard and Vassar Colleges and at the Dia Art Center. Day-trippers flock to antiques stores and galleries, not just in Hudson but also in Cold Spring and several other long-forgotten towns along the shoreline. Historical houses beckon: Olana and Cedar Grove are only two among hundreds that include the Rockefellers' residence (called Kykuit) and the renovated stone barns on the family estate at Pocantico Hills; designer Russel Wright's handsome Manitoga artfully sited in the woods near the Bear Mountain Bridge; and FDR's Hyde Park residence. Attendance figures are impressive, showing that the Walkway is hardly alone in attracting growing numbers of visitors to the region.

Hiking, rock climbing, biking, and boating opportunities abound in areas that might have been surrendered to sprawl. A new green mantle covers large stretches previously denuded for farming and logging. Home builders, buyers, and renters, daunted by crowding and steep prices in New York City and on Long Island and liberated by the Web from urban offices, have been snapping up old farmland and filling up new bars, cafes, and restaurants. Where citizens and leaders once turned their backs on the river, local waterfronts like that at Athens are being

17

revitalized. New ferry services now link towns on the river's west bank to New York City–bound Metro North and Amtrak trains on the other side. Never before has the region's great beauty, said by the original Baedeker travel guide to be "grander and more inspiring" than the Rhine itself, been so much appreciated by so many.

Earlier on, an alternative scenario beckoned as a growing population began to trample this hallowed ground. By the mid-twentieth century, after a long period of gradual environmental decline, the Hudson Valley could well have joined Long Island's Nassau County or its many New Jersey equivalents as quintessential "crudscape." Post–World War II growth patterns and the emergence of a suburban culture left a litter of dying towns abandoned when their industries became obsolete. Shopping malls cropped up on the peripheries. They contributed toxic runoff from highways and parking lots to the already unhealthy soup of untreated effluent entering the river and untreated emissions from poorly regulated factory pipelines. The river became a sewer. In 1969, wrote Robert Boyle in his celebrated book *The Hudson River: A Natural and Unnatural History*: "The Hudson River is the most beautiful, messed up, productive, ignored, and surprising piece of water on the face of the earth."

Much decay and poverty remains. The once-bountiful shad fishery has all but vanished, the victim of overharvesting and loss of spawning habitat along its historical migratory routes. Each May the tireless Hudson advocate Joan Davidson hosts what is now called the "shadless shad bake" for hundreds of devoted aficionados. Many other marine species continue to suffer from heavy doses of toxic pollution. Unsound development projects, often supported by local jurisdictions defying the concept of coordinated regional planning, result in pollution and needless sprawl. The current national economic crisis will impede progress and delay some initiatives. Nonetheless, this region has clearly turned the corner along the pathway toward revival and is undergoing a remarkable renaissance.

The Hudson Valley's passage from desolation to redemption begins with the bucolic and romantic years late in the nineteenth century, when some forward thinkers were already taking steps to protect a landscape they treasured. It encompasses the rise and fall of the industrial age. It moves on to the era of recovery that started about fifty years ago with a pivotal event: the seemingly endless seventeen-year struggle—fully won at last in 1981—to prevent Con Edison, the region's leading electric power company, from disfiguring scenic Storm King Mountain and killing millions of migrating fish by building a large plant on its flank. Since then, Hudson Valley citizens and leaders have scored countless victories in their quest to build a new society based on environmental and cultural values rather than on industry's grime. "Life's Hubbub Returns to Oft-Shunned Hudson," headlined the *New York Times*. Rip Van Winkle is up and at it.

Multiple forces have combined to bring about the currently brisk level of environmentally driven activity around the Hudson. Among them are the competitive energies of the valley's array of cultural institutions; the income-producing opportunities to revive waterfronts and abandoned lands along them; a proliferation of excellent privately run environmental organizations; a burst of creative private philanthropy; a buildup of infrastructure for a wide variety of recreational activities; the recent revival of family farming to supply healthy food for clamoring locavores; and occasional flickers of creative thought in Albany and Washington. This is a story less about the powerful galaxy of new institutions that enliven the valley than it is about the broad range of gifted people who have founded and nurtured them. Environmental advocates and professionals, politicians, community organizers, businesspeople, society ladies, cultural leaders, philanthropists, and committed ordinary citizens have all contributed to the development of this new economy and merit attention here.

A severe test of their values is also at hand. Almost all of the high-quality tap water enjoyed by eight million New York City residents and another million nearby comes from underground aquifers, rivers, and streams in the Catskill Mountains and the Delaware. Underlying much of this system, a mile down, is a huge layer of sedimentary rock called the Marcellus Shale, which, geologists have long known, contains vast quantities of natural gas, "trapped," says the private watchdog agency Riverkeeper, "between the layers of this fine-grained rock." In recent years gas companies have developed drilling techniques that now make it economical for them to exploit this resource. One is called fracturing, or "fracking," a noisy, messy process in which a mixture of water and sand, as well as increments of highly toxic chemicals that often including benzene, diesel fuel, or even nastier ingredients, is blasted at the rock to pry it loose and release the gas.

Severe environmental consequences for the fragile New York City watershed are widely feared if gas-drilling operations employing fracking, as commonly practiced in western and southern parts of the state and elsewhere in the country, are permitted to move eastward into extensive portions of the Catskills where the watershed and the northeastern end of the Marcellus overlap. Possible dangers include contamination of groundwater and surface water and air pollution with serious health implications. Public officials including Governor Andrew Cuomo have been wary. Riverkeeper and the Natural Resources Defense Council (NRDC) are conducting an aggressive antifracking campaign. Media coverage, including a major *New York Times* exposé that was seven months in the making and a poorly informed prodrilling reaction in the *New York Post,* fans the flames.

The stakes are high, with drilling advocates touting the huge windfall income their drilling leases generate for generally poor landowners and environmentalists warning of threats severe enough to "kill the Catskills," as one of them put it, and damage the New York City watershed severely enough to compel the United States Environmental Protection Agency (EPA) to take a drastic and long-feared step: require installation of a hugely expensive water filtration system. Public opinion splits sharply, with voices raised high at increasingly frequent hearings and debates on the subject. "This is the environmental issue of the century for New York State," said assembly member Barbara Lifton.

How this issue plays out will do much to reveal how firmly the transformative economy has pushed aside older and dirtier values in the Hudson Valley and become embedded. The seeds had been planted long before, within the region's splendid history—the tales well told and retold by countless authors about the colonial period, the Revolutionary War, the flowering of artists and writers of the nineteenth century. As for modern times, in his book *The Hudson: A History*, Tom Lewis found the river "more than ever the center of the nation's cultural geography" and

> *poised to enter a new era, one that would see, after a period of extraordinary pollution, an emphasis on recreation, conservation, preservation, the environment, and, for many, a transformation of the old order.*

What follows are many stories about how the region in recent years has labored with considerable success to recover its soul. I also reach beyond the region to show how such examples as the Walkway phenomenon and the city of Hudson's revival confirm a shift in thought and activity. Its components begin with an overarching idea, once largely confined to environmental nonprofits but now making headway among state and local agencies as well as public and private donors, that offers a big lesson for the nation. It is that in this place, where in many senses the environmental movement began in the 1960s, another giant step forward is also in progress.

Development in many Hudson Valley towns is now based on the once-radical idea that environmental protection, often won only after bitter struggles, can generate substantial economic and cultural benefits for communities and visitors. In former times, with environmental protection and economic progress widely seen as irreconcilable adversaries, each self-righteous camp fired withering salvos at the other. Later came less strident but still conventional calls for "balance" and for "sustainable development," the latter seen by some as an oxymoron, by others as a sound pathway toward economic progress. Now, the miracle of the Walkway, the city of Hudson's revival, and the flowering of the Hudson Valley overall show how protecting and restoring the environment there has in multiple respects emerged not just as the gentle handmaiden of sustainable development but as, ever more, the cutting edge of economic progress.

CHAPTER 2

Salad Days on the Mountain

ON A SUNNY SUMMER EVENING IN THE 1870S, ON THE WEST BANK OF the Hudson at Cornwall Landing in the Hudson Highlands, New York City looms as a distant glow, fifty-five miles downstream and out of sight behind the river's hilly Narrows. To the south in the foreground is thirteen-hundred-foot Storm King Mountain. This massive rounded hulk rises "like a brown bear out of the river," said Yale's legendary architecture professor Vincent J. Scully Jr., and presents itself as an "awesome" spectacle, "a primitive embodiment of the energies of the earth. It makes the character of wild nature physically visible in monumental form."

A hundred horse-drawn carriages are lined up at the Cornwall dock. Equestrians circulate. Dogs bark. Eyes turn southward as the spotless, flag-bedecked three-hundred-foot paddle wheel steamer *Mary Powell*, "Queen of the Hudson," comes into view as she continues her daily 3:30 p.m. run from Manhattan to the busy port of Kingston near Albany. Rounding the hulking mountain, the vessel glides into Newburgh Bay behind the capricious afternoon breeze and under the skilled guidance of Captain Absalom Anderson docks at the Village of Cornwall. The region's poet laureate, Nathaniel P. Willis, described the scene as "a gay pouring-down of visitors to the little dock." The buggies scoop up these hordes of disembarking passengers

23

and distribute them among what one local historian, Lewis Beach, described as the "scores" of hotels and boarding houses scattered along the hillsides of this verdant region.

The visitors had come to enjoy what the travel writer Paul Wilsack, in his 1933 book *Hudson River Landings*, called "the exhilarating effect of an entrancing variation of line and light and color," amid "the generally unspoiled primeval character of nature here, by the expanses of mountain-flank, by the silence of the currentless water, by the protective blue sky." Here "man dwells reticently, somewhat screened by the forest," Wilsack continued in a torrent of breathless prose echoing effusive sentiments that flourished during those times. Many observers, including especially Hudson River School painters such as Thomas Cole, John F. Kensett, Jasper F. Cropsey, Asher B. Durand, and Frederic Church, widely shared the author's belief in the beauty and goodness of nature, which, wrote art historian Barbara Babcock Lassiter, was for them a "spiritual necessity."

Storm King Mountain became an often-featured centerpiece in the painters' now, if not always, widely admired great panoramic landscape paintings. Transcendentalist authors of the Romantic era, especially Ralph Waldo Emerson, added to the glow with equally passionate expressions of admiration for what God had wrought along the Hudson's shores and outcries calling for the preservation of pristine wilderness. "America is a poem in our eyes," Emerson wrote. "Its ample geography dazzles the imagination." Washington Irving's Rip Van Winkle called the Catskills "fairy mountains" where "every change of season, every change of weather, indeed every hour of the day, produced some change in the magical hues and shapes of these mountains."

In his 1981 book *American Sublime*, Raymond J. O'Brien called the valley "a framed piece of the world" and "nature's greatest panorama," which "possessed that contradictory duality of aesthetics and industry . . . whose history is written in smoke, brick, steam, and rail— yet somehow a river of constant beauty." Artists grudgingly conceded the increasing importance of the river as a transportation corridor: The painter John F. Kensett showed steamboats in his work. But, reported Vassar College geographer Harvey Flad at a 2011 symposium entitled "Framing the Landscape," depictions of the commercial traffic tended to merge into a "poetic vision" of untrammeled landscape.

From these roots came a vocabulary that helped define the romantic visions that were fashionable at the time. "Sublime," says author Frances Dunwell in her wide-ranging book *The Hudson: America's River*, denoted "unpredictable" and "wild aspects of nature that showed God's power." The word "picturesque" was applied to calmer pastoral scenes featuring domestic animals, farmland, and gardens but ones Dunwell characterizes as "irregular, designed to heighten the sense of power in nature's struggle with opposing forces—the upheaval of mountains by convulsion and valleys broken by chasms." To this tumult the influential landscape architect Andrew Jackson Downing added the word "beautiful," a quality to be achieved through easy, flowing curves, soft surfaces, and rich, luxuriant growth.

Houses within these carefully arranged picturesque or beautiful landscapes would vary depending on topography and taste but would generally resemble gingerbread-y European styles, from the Gothic or Old English to the classically Italian, Tuscan, or Venetian. Adorning the grounds would be pathways, gently flowing streams or waterfalls, carefully sited trees, and rustic furniture. Views would lead from these semiconfined spaces to the meadows and hills beyond, the places that environmental historian David Stradling finds endowed with "the power of sublime nature in the mountains."

Washington Irving and James Fenimore Cooper, among many intellectual notables of the mid-nineteenth century, traveled Germany's storied Rhine. They and others pointed out similarities between it and the Hudson: Both rivers rise in the mountains. Both flow through hilly country, have narrow gorges, are renowned in romantic literature, and give off airs of mystery and legend. Artist Asher B. Durand wrote of the picturesque dwellings rising on the Hudson's shores as echoing the "feudal castles which still frown from the rocky banks of the Rhine."

While many later commentators returned to these themes and called the Hudson "America's Rhineland," others turned the tables. The Hudson is wider and deeper, the shoreline mountains higher, the scenery grander, said Hudson boosters. Read a 1852 essay in the *New York Times* in response to Thomas Cole's effusive descriptions of the Rhine: "Build a few old ruins on the Highland crests, and the supremacy in magnificent beauty will universally be yielded to our nation's hills." Reviewing the bidding in a 1939 photo essay, *Life* magazine concluded that "If anything, the comparison flatters the German river." Yet the passage of both rivers from a romantic past, through the rise and fall of heavy industry and accompanying pollution, to a new era of redemption, justifies the use of the admittedly incomplete analogy.

If appreciation of beauty lured spiritually motivated visitors to Cornwall and the surrounding countryside of the Hudson Valley, other considerations beckoned as well. One was comfort, with a prominent Cornwall booster, the poet Nathaniel Parker Willis, urging New Yorkers to enjoy a "sojourn far from the steaming metropolis." You eat and sleep better there, it was widely claimed. More serious a matter was health, with author Lewis Beach stating that "victims of phtisis [tuberculosis] by scores and hundreds have flocked to Cornwall and have experienced the most favorable results." Excellent drinking water for New York City became available as early as 1842, via an aqueduct from the Croton River, a Hudson tributary, which offered a welcome alternative to earlier sources so vile that not even animals would use them. Even so, fears arising from occasional cholera and typhoid outbreaks had prompted many New Yorkers to flee from fouled drinking water at times, and the Hudson Valley was a frequent destination. And there was of course recreation, with mountain hiking trails to be explored; streams, ponds, and lakes, as well as the river, for swimming and fishing; and ice boating during the colder winters of earlier times. Beach could hardly contain himself, applauding Cornwall for

> *the salubrity of its air, the diversity of its scenery, the fruitfulness of its soil, the beauty of its lakes, the grandeur of its mountains, the quiet splendor of its dales, the magnificence of its slopes and ridges, the superiority and abundance of its water, its economic advantages, manufacturing facilities, mineral developments and agricultural resources, its Revolutionary association, and wealth in historical and traditional incident.*

While increasing numbers of day-trippers and vacationers jostled into the Hudson Valley's public space as the city expanded and its population grew, much of the choicest land along the river's banks had long since fallen into the hands of a few wealthy and powerful families. In the aftermath of Henry Hudson's Dutch-sponsored exploration of the river in 1609 aboard the aging but plucky little sixty-five-foot *Half Moon*, and the declaration of a new Dutch province called New Netherland, a polyglot assortment of "patroons" began to occupy Hudson Valley land sold to them by administrators in Manhattan. Among these was pearl merchant Kiliaen van Rensselaer, who acquired a huge tract called Rensselaerwick that encompassed what are now the twin cities of Albany and Troy.

After only fifty-five years of Dutch control of the region, the British amicably took over in 1664, arguing that discoveries of John Cabot and

Captain John Smith predating Hudson's excursion gave them a legitimate claim. Many of the upriver Dutch settlers stayed on, as Rensselaerwick became a manor under the British system of permanent leases. Now they were joined by British neighbors. Robert Livingston, the first of a large family of that name to occupy Hudson Valley lands, came by a tract spread across 160,000 acres, including some ten miles of riverfront on the east bank south of Albany. Total Livingston holdings reached more than one million acres, says Dennis Delafield, a descendant.

British and Dutch intermarried, forming something of a multinational Hudson elite linking endless Livingstons with Schuylers and van Rensselaers and Philipses and others from privileged families. Palatinate Germans were there as well and French Huguenots. These people formed a quaint society built around garden parties and dances, charades, musicales, and picnics. They remained aloof from the changes that came with the Industrial Revolution and the hurly-burly of the teeming masses of Irish and Italians and Swedes crowding into New York City. A high priest of the Hudson at mid-nineteenth century was the highly influential landscape gardener Andrew Jackson Downing of Newburgh. His designs, reported Carl Carmer in his classic 1939 book *The Hudson,* often embraced Gothic elements—urns, statues, weeping fountains, prospect towers, pavilions, bridges, rustic seats, and rockwork. Downing's customers were "the prosperous merchants of the Hudson River country," Carmer continued. "They talked learnedly of Tuscan villas, Tudor mansions, Mansard dwellings, Gothic cottages." Downing died in 1852 at the age of only thirty-five, drowned while trying to save family members and others aboard the furiously burning steamer *Henry Clay,* aground near Riverdale after fire broke out amidships. Tributes to the fallen aesthete gushed in from all over. "It was as if the rumble of an upriver thunderstorm had silenced the festival of roses," wrote Carmer,

And all the guests knew they would be scattered soon. Only for a little while longer the ladies of the river houses looked out from the belvederes and gazebos that crowned their undulant acres of lawn and trees and sighed for the proud dark man who had made them beautiful. A little while longer they played sad songs upon their harps, remembering him in their moonlit pavilions.

The opulent age lasted until well after the turn of the century, as Rockefellers began to occupy Pocantico Hills, the family compound near Tarrytown, and Perkinses gathered at Wave Hill in Riverdale. Plutocrat banker J. P. Morgan plied the river aboard his famous yacht the *Corsair* en route to and from Cragston, his Victorian mansion in Highland Falls near West Point, a few miles south of Storm King Mountain. Another Hudson baron, banker James P. Stillman, when departing the grounds for the morning boat ride to his office at the First National City Bank in New York City from his eight-hundred-acre spread in Cornwall, was known to muster family and servants to stand in formation to undergo military-style 8:00 a.m. inspections. Close by were Osborns, Harrimans of the Union Pacific railroad family, Vanderbilts, and Roosevelts. Along "Millionaire's Row" on the river's east bank, one of the newly rich built a replica of the Petit Trianon, Marie Antoinette's nature retreat on the grounds of Versailles, Carl Carmer reported. Another launched a Florentine castle but stopped when his money ran out.

Edith Wharton, novelist of high society and its excesses, drew inspiration from this region's history. Her book *Hudson River Bracketed* (1929), while not her most successful work, is notable for having been named after a style championed by the architect Alexander Jackson Davis that was in vogue during the mid-nineteenth century. The fictional Willows, a Dutchess County house that was built in that manner with "architectural elements ingeniously combined from the Chinese and the Tuscan," plays a major role in Wharton's story about a star-crossed lover and his Hudson Valley travails. The novel is replete with references to Coleridge and to William Cullen Bryant and Washington Irving, both said to have visited the home of the elite family around which the story revolved. Our hero Vance Weston has a predawn tryst near the Willows with Halo Spear of the region's dominant family, and the passionate scene is presented in this way:

> *Then Miss Spear, laying her hand on Vance's shoulder, turned him about toward a break in the swarthy fell of the eastern mountains, and through it came the red edge of the sun. They watched in silence as it hung there apparently unmoving; then they glanced away for a moment, and when they looked back they saw that it had moved; saw the forerunning glow burn away the ashen blur in the forest hollows, the upper sky whiten, and the daylight take possession of the air. Again they turned westward, looking toward the Hudson, and now the tawny suffusion was drawing down the slopes of the farther shore, till gradually, very gradually, the river hollows also were washed of their mists, and the great expanse of the river shone bright as steel in the clear shadow.*

Some of the gentry were abruptly awakened from their long swoon when quarrying operations affecting life in the lower Hudson Valley commenced just before the end of the nineteenth century. For decades advertisers had been painting the lower Hudson River's stately Palisades, thirty miles of vertical cliff reaching a height of 550 feet, with advertising signs. Then came quarrymen, blasting the diabase cliffs and transporting the crumbled rock across the river for construction projects. Dynamiting the wall made a racket, fouled the air, shook the earth, triggered clouds of dust, and seriously debased the appearance of cliffs much admired in visitors' accounts dating back to that written by Henry Hudson's seaman scribe Robert Juet about the *Half Moon*'s 1609 expedition.

Protests against the quarrying, which began with actions taken by a group of women in Englewood, a New Jersey suburb a few miles west of the cliffs, got nowhere until the issue came to the attention of outdoorsman and conservation enthusiast Theodore Roosevelt. In 1899, when he became New York State's governor, he came to think that buying the Palisades would be a bully idea. Business nabobs, fed up with the noise and the disfigurement of the splendid cliffs, chimed in, supporting the idea of preserving this landscape, which represented what geographer Harvey Flad described as a "core value" for the region. The banker John Pierpont Morgan, who had viewed with dismay the results of the quarrying from the bridge of the *Corsair*, pushed the highly effective insurance czar (later a Morgan associate) George W. Perkins of Wave Hill to lead the effort to save the cliffs.

In 1900 New Jersey governor Foster M. Voorhees had also become persuaded that preserving the Palisades scenery would be good for both states. Bills creating the Palisades Interstate Park and a governing Palisades Interstate Park Commission were duly passed in both Albany and Trenton. Roosevelt dragooned Perkins into becoming the commission's founding chairman. By the end of that year, after some tough negotiating with the quarrymen, dynamiting of the New Jersey palisades stopped. It was what Robert O. Binnewies, who later served for ten years (1990–2000) as the park's superintendent and wrote the book *Palisades: 100,000 Acres in 100 Years*, called a "wonderful holiday gift for thousands of Hudson River Valley residents." Wrote one Albert Shaw in the *American Monthly*: "The Palisades have been rescued before the harm done to them has been irreparable. It's a pity the mischief went as far as it did."

In his book Binnewies details how through painstaking negotiations and manipulations the Palisades Interstate Park system grew and flourished, providing protection for the New York City watershed and its impressive biodiversity, and recreational opportunities for city dwellers. It would become a wonderful haven for "city waifs," said Perkins. Protection of parklands would also guard them from what forester and early conservationist Gifford Pinchot later called "ruthless and indiscriminate cutting and destruction," propelling the nation toward "timber famine." A noteworthy section of the Binnewies book shows how railroad baron Edward H. Harriman, working with then governor Charles Evans Hughes and other property owners, began to fulfill the vision of preserving as wild and scenic a vast block of land from the Hudson westward to New Jersey's Ramapo and encompassing West Point. Harriman died in 1909, but his widow Mary carried on with the process that eventually incorporated 46,613 acres of invaluable Harriman land into the park. Mrs. Harriman also donated millions of dollars toward the park's maintenance and expansion. The quid pro quo: The state acceded to a Harriman request that it stop building a prison planned for nearby and relocate it to where "it will not interfere with the plans and purposes" of the park. Looking back decades later, New York megaplanner Robert Moses characterized the gift as "a piece of statesmanship and philanthropy so far-sighted that few people understood its significance."

No Hudson Valley leader of the time was more passionate in his advocacy of measures to preserve the magnificent vistas gracing the Hudson Highlands and make their woodlands available for nature education and recreation than obstetrician Edward Lasell Partridge. From his ample gray house in Cornwall-on-Hudson, on the north-facing slope of Storm King Mountain, the elegantly bearded Dr. Partridge and his frequent weekend visitors enjoyed a sweeping view across landscaped grounds designed by Frederick Law Olmsted, to the cliffs of the Shawangunks on the skyline. Guests included Dr. Partridge's good friend, the author Joseph Conrad. Surrounded by nymph sculptures, they swam in a pool built of local rock, played tennis on a court tucked into the hillside, and roamed the mountain's trails on foot or horseback. Photo albums from the era display many shots of horses and buggies, canoes, catboats, dancing.

While the guests and neighbors played, Partridge thought hard about the preservation of the magnificent scenery that surrounded them. In a benchmark 1907 article in *Outlook* magazine, he proposed that a 125-square-mile portion of the Highlands, on both sides of the river, be converted through land condemnation into a federal government preserve, adding the heart of the region to the growing system of national parks that already included Yosemite and Yellowstone. "Every foreign visitor to the United States comes with the purpose of seeing the most beautiful river of North America," he said, and making the Highlands a national park would protect them before more damage was done. He proposed that the park span sixty-five square miles, with the Narrows as its anchor.

Passionate about his dream, Partridge lobbied it hard with politicians, high-society friends and colleagues in New York and upriver, and the media. He attracted widespread support. "That these Hudson River Highlands ought to be availed of and made a world-wide attraction like the Falls of Niagara or Yellowstone Park there is no doubt," wrote one correspondent. "Nor is there any doubt that some day it will be done."

During his tour of duty as the first chief of the nation's Forest Service, Gifford Pinchot took Partridge to see President Theodore Roosevelt, who "gave every evidence of support." Others chimed in. "No woods, no water supply," said one newspaper, arguing that the "water horsepower" of New York was "of greater value commercially than all the coal mines of Pennsylvania" but would remain so "only if the forests which stored the water were preserved." But despite a blizzard of correspondence, the drafting of bills, and much encouragement, the initiative on the federal level eventually failed in 1907 for want of money and broad political support.

New York State was more cooperative, creating Bear Mountain State Park in 1909 and later helping to assemble a choice array of other Highlands properties that were eventually absorbed into the fast-growing Palisades Interstate Park system or as portions of the Hudson Highlands State Park along the river's east bank. Foreshadowing the burst of highly creative private philanthropy that came much later in the twentieth century, Perkins generated millions of dollars for the system in donations from grandee families lining the river's banks. Railroader and Wall Street investor William H. Osborn, who built several castles in the Highlands, was another who acted on his belief in "saving God's scenery," as Bill Moyers put it in a 2002 television special. He did much to protect choice parklands in his hills above Garrison on the river's eastern shore.

So Dr. Partridge's plea for a protected Highlands was in fact achieved, though not in the form that he envisioned. After seventeen years of service as a commissioner of the Palisades Interstate Park, Partridge died in 1930. For many years thereafter, his house with its expansive view remained empty but in place, a proud symbol of a grand era, until it was declared unsafe and a fire hazard by its owner, the nearby Storm King School. The house was bulldozed down in 1986 and buried on the mountain's west-facing slope.

Suggestions of the Partridge lifestyle are to be found in a relatively modest red house, a short distance downhill from where his mansion stood, now owned by members of the Stowell family. Esty Stowell, a pipe-smoking advertising executive who spoke wisely in short, carefully fashioned phrases, and Hellie, his stylish wife who cared passionately for the natural world, led a carefully mannered life in Cornwall that was in large measure built around reverence for the past. The house, something of a time warp, is kept largely in its late-nineteenth- and early-twentieth-century condition with memorabilia-lined walls, bookshelves replete with classic Hudson volumes, and vintage prints and paintings. Antique appliances, still working, adorn a handsome kitchen. A 1936 Ford woody station wagon rests in the garage.

The porch offers that same grand northward view that Dr. Partridge treasured. Nearby, at the edge of the meadow, are two wooden armchairs to which on warm evenings the Stowells would retreat, lovingly stirred martinis in hand, to enjoy the setting sun and the view. The origins of this house remain obscure, but for many years it was occupied by one Henrietta Fellowes, Esty Stowell's grandmother, who had arrived from New Orleans in the 1890s. With Mrs. Partridge often ailing, Henrietta remained Dr. Partridge's close friend and boon companion until her death in 1925. In his will Dr. Partridge gave her daughter, Esty Stowell's mother, first option to buy the house. She took up the offer, says Esty's son Frank Stowell, "and the rest is a lucky history for us."

The next generation of Stowells are conservationists as passionate and generous as were their turn-of-the century forebears. My wife Flo and I were touched when the Stowells' offspring—sons Frank and Esty Jr. and daughters Lally and Jenipher—offered us the use of the classic Red House that they still own as a base for my travels while researching this book. Taking up this option, we on two occasions in 2010 slipped back into the world of a century ago, little changed on the shoulder of Storm King Mountain.

For me it was a rediscovery, for my appreciation of the Hudson Highlands goes back to an earlier time. After World War II broke out in Europe, my patriotic British parents, US residents since the early 1930s, sought to respond to the call of duty. A Royal Navy officer during World War I, my father was deemed too old to go back to sea. Instead, he joined British Security Coordination, a spy network designed to help foster Anglo-American espionage cooperation and do its best to keep the Yanks on the right side. His boss was the trim "Quiet Canadian," Sir William Stephenson, the "Little Bill" counterpart to "Big Bill," Major General "Wild Bill" Donovan, who later headed the tweedy, spooky Office of Strategic Services. My mother helped organize transatlantic convoys.

New York City residents when war broke out, during the war my parents moved many times up and down the eastern seaboard, from Ottawa to Charleston, South Carolina. My two much-older brothers were long gone from the nest. Mike, the oldest, flew for Britain's Fleet Air Arm and much later served a stretch as President George H. W. Bush's secretary of the US Army. Searching for a means of keeping me out of harm's way during those uncertain times, my wandering parents discovered the classics teacher Malcolm Gordon. He had founded the little boarding school in Garrison, New York, that bore his name, in an old house with a Hudson view. In fall 1941, aged seven, I was enrolled. I distinctly remember the formidable Mrs. Gordon assembling the entire student body of twenty or so boys and informing us that the Japanese had bombed Pearl Harbor. We studied Latin, climbed the hillsides, collected salamanders in ponds, and developed a primitive view of the wonders of nature. On Sundays, dressed in our signature gray flannel trousers and blue blazers with the heavily encrusted school badge sewn to the breast pocket, we marched down the road to St. Andrew's Church and recited the school psalm, number 121, which aptly begins:

I will lift up mine eyes unto the hills
From whence cometh my help

I remained at that little school for three academic years, until it was compelled to close for want of teachers (when all had been drafted), food, and fuel for supply vehicles. Much later, sheer happenstance drew me back to the Highlands. Our close friends Herschel and Peggy Post, who lived close to us on New York's West Eighty-Eighth Street, had purchased a small house just below the Partridge estate on Cornwall's Mountain Road. It was a short distance downhill from the Stowells' Red House and within easy walking distance from a number of other grand houses and the rusticators within them. The summit of famous Storm King Mountain was a brisk forty-five-minute climb away.

In 1973, when Herschel's employer sent the Posts off for a tour of duty in Brussels, we rented their little house. Subsequently, we bought one of our own, also sited near Storm King Mountain. Neighbors included Beatrice ("Smokey") Duggan and her husband Stephen—she a dedicated conservationist, he a New York lawyer so fiercely competitive that each year, when he was older and could not run, he would pitch for both teams at the annual all-ages community softball game. That way, defying the traditional custom of disregarding the actual numbers and declaring the final score a tie, he could always claim to have been on the winning side.

We spent our weekends reveling in the beauty surrounding us—hiking in the forests, picnicking, playing tennis, canoeing, gardening, ice skating and playing hockey on the ponds, cross-country skiing, swimming in a community pool filled with local water of immaculate purity, gathering chanterelles from a secret place on its grounds. Migrating warblers, bright in the spring, adorned the grove of large oaks near the house. The black-and-white was always the first arrival. I found an old trove of peonies hidden in a briar patch and brought them to light. We read the old Beach and Willis books that graced the Stowell library and that of another close neighbor: witty Curt Muser, owner of yet another classic shingled house on "the mountain" that dates back to early in the twentieth century. Curt's music-loving wife Frani was a Vassar classmate of the novelist Mary McCarthy. The Musers' friends included Elizabeth Bishop, Aaron Copland, John Cage, and Merce Cunningham. Cage crept in periodically to gather wild mushrooms, which, we were informed, he sold in New York to supplement his income, which remained modest long after he became famous.

As late as the mid-twentieth century and even more recently, it was tempting for many Hudsonians and visitors to enjoy the aesthetics and comforts of Hudson Valley life as we did, in the manner of Dr. Partridge's weekend guests or Edith Wharton's lovestruck characters or the Musers' distinguished visitors. Those who fought to "save" the region remained prompted more by scenery and landscape considerations than by the growing need to safeguard an environment that was becoming ever more degraded. Scientific knowledge remained scant, and early warnings from Rachel Carson and other pioneer researchers were widely ridiculed. But as the degree of environmental damage that had already been done to the valley grew ever more apparent, and as the threats to already weakened lands and waters became ever more ominous, it was not long before the region's conservationists found themselves striving to protect not only carefully selected viewsheds but an entire ecosystem that had long been under heavy attack. In this transition our neighbors the Duggans were early adopters.

CHAPTER 3

Storm Clouds, Clearing Skies

BACK IN THOSE NINETEENTH-CENTURY YEARS OF MELLOW RECREATION for the most privileged Hudsonians, dramatic environmental deterioration swirled around them, thanks to a rough-and-ready industrial economy that was brazenly taking shape along the river. Early on, woodsmen had stripped the tidy Hudson Valley of trees to meet the growing demand for ships' spars, telegraph and telephone poles, railroad ties, building materials, and charcoal. Erosion was one consequence. Brickyards and foundries proliferated, and so did dusty cement plants, the smoke from their high-temperature kilns fouling the air. Later came factories of many sorts, power plants, metalworking shops, pulp and textile mills. Water pollution ensued, especially around towns such as Troy, just north of Albany, which—with no opposition—dumped raw sewage into the river and its tributaries. "Open sewers from that city face upon the river like so many giant backsides," wrote the fiery Robert Boyle.

After World War II sprawl began to engulf some locations, bringing with it an increase in toxic runoff from highways, parking lots, and chemical-drenched industrial farms. The precious watershed serving millions of users in New York City and environs, famous for the quality of its product, faced new threats. Industries deliberately selected riverside plant locations for the convenience of dumping raw wastes overboard. You could, it was often said, tell the color of the cars being painted at General Motors' Chevrolet assembly plant in Sleepy Hollow, which operated from 1914 to 1996, by looking at the adjacent water.

As late as the 1980s, a private nonprofit group called INFORM showed how persistent the river's pollution problems had become. The organization's team worked stubbornly to quantify the toxic pollution entering the river from point sources (drainpipes) or in the form of unchanneled "nonpoint" runoff. Sifting through masses of official data that it described as "incomplete, inconsistent, and confusing," INFORM was nonetheless able to come up with alarming information about the extent of the problem and the inadequacy of regulatory mechanisms at the time. Thanks to heavy discharges of toxic chemicals from industrial sources, many not listed on federal or state permits, the Hudson had become "a classic example of river pollution by hazardous chemicals." The striped bass fishery, once commercially important, had been entirely shut down because of this contamination. Migratory shad, long heralded as a highlight of the annual food cycle for its tasty roe, all but vanished from Hudson habitats. Health officials warned against eating nine major species found in the lower Hudson.

The seven known or suspected carcinogens included in INFORM's survey were released from plants located in sixty-eight jurisdictions with a combined population of over 1,270,000. Plants operated by twenty-two industrial companies discharged five or more of the toxins surveyed, with IBM and two other companies each discharging fourteen different toxins. In his preface to the second volume of INFORM's report, published in 1987, Gene Likens of the New York Botanical Garden's Institute of Ecosystem Studies was moved to ask a bracing question: "Can we continue to use one of this nation's most important natural resources as a cesspool?" At the *New Yorker,* publisher of Rachel Carson's powerful *Silent Spring,* E. B. White pledged the magazine would "assemble bulletins tracing Man's progress in making the planet uninhabitable."

During the 1950s, a period when the river and its shores were still being severely abused, the Hudson's gentry remained largely unaware of how serious the situation had become. What did finally stir them up was initially not a pollution issue but a dispute over scenery reminiscent of the turn-of-the-century battle to save the Palisades from the quarrymen. It was the titanic, seventeen-year struggle involving the power company Con Edison's 1963 proposal to the Federal Power Commission (now the Federal Energy Regulatory Commission or FERC) to build a giant pumped-storage hydropower plant on the very Storm King Mountain that had, since Revolutionary War times, been revered as the keystone of America's Rhineland. During off-peak hours at night, Con Edison's giant pumps would suck up river water and park it a thousand feet above sea level in a 260-acre reservoir (the world's biggest, with a peak capacity of twelve billion gallons) near the mountain. During the daytime this water would be released through turbines to give New York City's power grid a boost at peak usage times for office buildings. From an engineering standpoint the plan seemed feasible and more practical than deploying gas turbines for the same purpose. For Motton L. Waring, the company's vice president for engineering, it represented the capstone of a long and faithful career.

For many reasons the proposal also raised hackles. Strong voices echoed earlier times in the valley by objecting to the project on strictly aesthetic grounds. The plant would form a hideous gash across the face of the very mountain that Hudson River School artists of the nineteenth century most fervently admired and painted, it was argued. Testimony came from cultural spokespeople such as Yale's architecture professor Vincent Scully and theater critic Brooks Atkinson. They and others raised objections to the idea of defacing the most beautiful section of the river by installing power transmission lines above the classic Bear Mountain Bridge. During the battle Randall LeBoeuf, Con Ed's top lawyer, had scornfully referred to opponents as "birdwatchers." He had generated guffaws and lively opposition by testifying that the project would actually enhance the region's beauty.

Environmentally, though this was not a major factor early in the struggle, the risks were also high. Experts came forward with evidence about the great harm that the pumping and warming of the plant's water would do to populations of striped bass and other prominent migratory fish for which the Narrows and adjacent waters represent important spawning habitat. Many fish would be sucked into the system and pulverized, forming a noxious gurry in the pipeline. Those people and organizations concerned with the quality and quantity of New York City's drinking water worried that constructing Con Edison's power transmission lines could damage the underwater pipeline that crosses the river at Cornwall and carries 40 percent of that drinking water down from the Catskills. The pipeline had been drilled through stubborn bedrock and completed in 1914 only after severe hardship.

As chronicled in great detail in Allan R. Talbot's *Power along the Hudson*, despite the hazards noted above, the proposal generated support from many key sectors. Nelson Rockefeller, New York State's governor at the time, was a great believer in big infrastructure projects. Along with his brother Laurance, he had championed an unsuccessful effort to build a six-lane Hudson River Expressway along the Hudson's east bank from Manhattan to Croton. The motive, some said, was to enhance the value of the thirty-six-hundred-acre family estate at Pocantico Hills. Early on, the Rockefellers also favored Con Edison's Storm King proposal, sympathizing with Con Edison's desperate need for new energy sources to respond to New York City's insatiable thirst for more power to supply air-conditioning systems. To speed the approval process at the Federal Power Commission, Governor Rockefeller installed his like-minded cousin, Alexander Aldrich, as director of the pivotal Hudson River Valley Commission. This body would have preferred a location other than Storm King for the new power plant, said the governor, but would settle for Storm King if no better site could be found.

Laurance Rockefeller, whose status as a leading national conservationist had won him widespread and well-deserved admiration, carefully maneuvered his way through the Storm King debate. He affirmed in 1964 his belief in the desirability of "multiple use" for the mountain and its environs and echoed his brother in stating that he would support the project unless a better way to feed power to the city could be found. "Given the hard fact of the proposal," he wrote one skeptic, Chauncey Stillman of the Cornwall banking family, in August 1964, "we felt it would be better to work with the company's own estimate of the effect of the project on the landscape, rather than to oppose it outright with no assurance of success."

At the outset of the multiyear debate, the Palisades Interstate Park Commission that Laurance Rockefeller dominated indicated support for the company's proposal. Cornwall residents, drawn to the prospect of jobs at Con Ed and company promises to bolster a weak local economy, lined up solidly in favor. The local mayor, Mike Donohue, expressed jubilation over new tax revenues that would underwrite many long-postponed civic improvements, including a renovation of the waterfront that had suffered badly from neglect after the glory years of the *Mary Powell*. Some were even led to think, Allan Talbot reported, that bringing Con Ed aboard would enable Cornwall to reduce to zero all taxes on residential property.

But alarmed reactions to Con Ed's proposal came from many quarters. Garden club members, environmentalists, and Robert Boyle and his colleagues at the Hudson River Fishermen's Association all protested vigorously. Vigilant citizens joined in. The Hudson River sloop *Clearwater*, built with leadership from the passionate folksinger Pete Seeger, plied the river in protest against Con Ed. A makeshift fifty-vessel flotilla, led by the America's Cup twelve-meter racing yacht *Weatherly*, owned by Chauncey Stillman, commodore of the New York Yacht Club, paraded upriver from New York City in September 1964 to picket the mountain. The stunt, cooked up by a public relations man, won a burst of favorable attention. Successive galaxies of top New York lawyers pitched in.

In 1965 the Federal Power Commission, weary of a sort of debate to which it was not accustomed, flatly waved off all objections. "Here the impact of the project on the surrounding area is minimal," it ruled, "while the need for electricity from this economical and dependable source is great." But this was hardly the end of the story: Ensuing litigation resulted in a dramatic victory for the opposition when at the end of 1965 a three-judge appeals panel affirmed the importance of scenic beauty; stated that the FPC had not provided convincing evidence on many points, including the hazards to fish; and blocked Con Edison from proceeding. The legal tussle droned on, focusing now not so much on the scenery issues as on the environmental impacts. It finally ended in a negotiated "Hudson River Peace Treaty," achieved in 1980 with former EPA administrator Russell E. Train as referee. Con Ed grudgingly surrendered its license to build the plant and donated the land it owned on the mountain to the state park system. In return, after another protracted struggle, the company achieved a major concession from the EPA, which dropped its requirement that Con Edison install expensive new closed-cycle water-cooling towers at three nearby nuclear power plants. The towers would have reduced fish kills by 95 percent, said the Riverkeeper organization.

The 1965 court ruling greatly enthused protagonists of environmental law, barely taking shape at the time, who correctly termed the

Storm King victories as of prime national significance. The court had accorded environmentalists the right to sue even though they had no economic stake in the outcome, considering them to be an "injured party" and according them "standing" on the grounds that they represented the public interest. In establishing this new precedent, the appeals court brought about what is widely considered to be "the birth of environmental law."

Storm King's importance extends well beyond the courtroom into broader sectors. Con Ed attorney LeBoeuf's attacks insulted and energized the formerly aloof Hudsonian patricians, and they became proactive in using money and power to guide the Hudson's future. They had been relatively passive during two world wars and the Depression of the 1930s. But in the 1960s, with a major scenery issue on the table, these people once again stepped forward. Echoing the values and concerns of the early twentieth century, following in the footsteps of Dr. Partridge, George W. Perkins, and E. H. Harriman, more and more of them became awakened, empowered, and emboldened. They were indefatigable letter writers themselves—few top newspaper and television editors escaped their notice—and the public relations campaign that they fashioned was a model of sophistication and energy for its time. They saw the Con Edison proposal, said geographer Harvey Flad, as no less than an affront to the entire nation's cultural identity.

Esty and Hellie Stowell were among the aggrieved. So were Stephen and Smokey Duggan, whose nearby residence was set in deep oak woods, offering a splendid view westward toward the mountains. With strong-willed grace, flashing bright blue eyes, and a long family history in the region, Smokey Duggan did not hesitate to align herself with the opposition. Eventually, she reeled in her husband, a New York City litigator known for his tenacity in arguing tough cases for corporate clients. The *New York Times* published her strongly worded letter, which she signed with her maiden name to avoid embarrassing him. A neighbor on the mountain, the elegant Pierre Ledoux, fired off salvos of letters to state and federal officials and politicians. Together with other leaders, several of whom also maintained residences on Storm King Mountain above Cornwall, this group founded the Scenic Hudson Preservation Conference as the nonprofit organization to lead the charge against Con Edison.

"I speak not as an expert but simply as a resident of Cornwall, New York, of five generations standing," Smokey Duggan testified at a 1965 Federal Power Commission hearing. "My grandfather, then a struggling minister, chose Cornwall as his living place because of the great splendor of the Hudson gorge at Storm King Mountain. Today this corridor still remains as one of our few great scenic and historical areas in the entire east. Today it is still viewed by boatloads of wondering tourists." She went on to enumerate the ways in which the Con Edison project was an environmental hazard. It would, she said, "spell the doom of this great corridor," destroying the town's best reservoir, which had been donated by her grandmother and which Con Edison would pump "full of polluted water from the Hudson River." She also complained bitterly that "the tactics used in some of these industrial land grabs undermine the democratic process." In particular she was referring to the stealthy passage, in 1963, of a Cornwall ordinance allowing "a Mayor or Town Board to sell or give away the water resources of their community without a public referendum." (This was the maneuver that had incensed Steve Duggan, prompting him to join his wife in the struggle to save the mountain.) In closing, Smokey Duggan invoked then President Lyndon B. Johnson, who had said that "Man should be served and not intimidated by modern technology."

The "standing" accorded environmental groups in the 1965 Storm King ruling led to the creation and rapid growth of many of them. Some of those who had launched the Scenic Hudson Preservation Conference went on to found what became the now globally powerful Natural Resources Defense Council. Within the region, the retitled Scenic Hudson grew steadily in influence and direct accomplishment; I was privileged to serve on its board for several years. The Open Space Institute, launched in 1964 as a statewide corollary to the Scenic Hudson Preservation Conference, continues to enjoy inspired leadership and, using great creativity in stitching together packages of funding, claims to have protected one hundred thousand acres of land. Local land trusts have blossomed in a number of communities. In recent years, for example, the staff of the Hudson Highlands Land Trust has more than tripled. Its program now encompasses not just land preservation but also education activities and involvement in public policy issues, down to the nub of it all, zoning. The region teems with ad hoc alliances, coalitions, and groups advocating sustainable development and organic farming.

Having standing in court challenged the Hudson's more aggressive environmental groups such as Clearwater, the Hudson River Fishermen's Association, and the new Riverkeeper organization to test their new muscles vis-à-vis the polluters. Early in the 1970s, with politicians gradually catching on to the fact that something was going terribly awry with the environment, a flurry of legislative activity at the federal level saw the birth of key new pieces of legislation: the Clean Air and Clean Water Acts and the National Environmental Policy Act. With the EPA newly empowered to clamp down, it became increasingly difficult for industrial polluters to behave as they long had on the Hudson and elsewhere. Many court victories were racked up, and in the aftermath of mandated cleanup operations, gains were scored.

Local fisherman, boatbuilder, and streetwise Irishman John Cronin became Riverkeeper and quickly gained fame by maneuvering a small boat to catch oil tankers that anchored upstream to rinse their oil tanks and discharge the polluted rinse water overboard. The Hudson Riverkeeper was the first of what are now hundreds of such organizations the world over that maintain a keen lookout for violators of antipollution regulations. Lawyer and activist Robert F. Kennedy Jr. founded this organization and remains chair of its coordinating body, the Waterkeeper Alliance.

No industrial project on the Hudson presented more of an environmental hazard than the two plants that General Electric built in 1947, in the adjacent towns of Fort Edward and Hudson Falls north of Albany. During one stage of building electrical goods such as capacitors and transformers for industrial use, these products were bathed in an oily liquid containing polychlorinated biphenyls (PCBs)—industrial chemicals that were highly toxic though widely used for insulation. After the vats were lifted out, reported Michael Rivlin in the *Amicus Journal*,

> *the oil that clung to their exteriors was washed away into the factory's wastewater and then, untreated, into the river. About 130 million pounds of PCBs were used at the two sites, of which about 1.1 million pounds were discharged into the river.*

PCBs were used in this manner over the course of thirty years, until they were finally banned in 1977. During the lifetime of this ugly process, scientists were learning in ever more sobering detail about the health hazards posed by the PCBs, stubborn substances that degrade only very slowly and linger in ever-higher concentrations while moving up the food chain toward ingestion by human beings. Studies of PCB accumulation in fish led to evidence that they cause cancer in those fish and that human consumption of PCB-laced fish can lead to learning difficulties, endocrine disruption, and various forms of cancer, including non-Hodgkin's lymphoma. Wrote Robert F. Kennedy Jr. and John Cronin in their 1997 book *The Riverkeepers:* "The public's hopes, raised so high by the Hudson's improvement, were replaced by fear that the river had become a toxic threat."

Once PCBs were classified by the EPA as a "probable human carcinogen," there commenced a long and complex series of court battles over what to do about these highly persistent poisons. Measures taken included fishing bans or restrictions along various parts of the river and the designation of a two-hundred-mile stretch of the river—all the way down to New York City, where sediments containing PCBs were found—as a Superfund site. With GE for years contesting that the best way to handle the PCBs was to leave them alone on the seafloor, the EPA pressed for dredging operations, which after protracted negotiations finally got underway in May 2009 and are expected to carry on for five to seven years.

Those looking for leadership from the Rockefellers on Hudson Valley environmental issues were sometimes rewarded, sometimes not. Often the family remained on the sidelines about Hudson conservation issues, never quite persuaded that in many senses environmental protection would become the key to the valley's economic development. As evidenced by the positions they took on the expressway and Con Edison issues, the Rockefeller family sometimes seemed to put business or personal interests first. Some family members were content to enjoy the region's comforts from within their compound at Pocantico Hills. With its own stables, golf course, and "playhouse" with tennis courts and a pool, the estate enabled them to relax in gated seclusion with carefully selected invited guests (I remember as a teenager early in the 1950s driving there to a dance in my decrepit 1934 Ford coupe, miraculously being waved through the checkpoint and wafted into a dream world of great style and beauty).

To be sure, Laurance Rockefeller led a battle to halt an effort by Central Hudson, the local power company, to build a pumped storage power plant at the already heavily quarried Breakneck Ridge in Cold Spring on the river's east bank opposite Storm King. Central Hudson relented in 1967, when the Rockefeller family's Jackson Hole Preserve Inc. bought the thirty-five-hundred-acre site and established it as the original portion of what later became the Hudson Highlands State Park. Laurance's son Larry was a staunch toiler at the Natural Resources Defense Council for twenty-five years. Laurance's daughter Dr. Lucy Waletzky became a popular and respected voice in the environmental community, developing a deep interest in New York's extensive but underfunded network of state parks. For years she has served with distinction and generosity as board chair of the state Council of Parks, Recreation, and Historic Preservation.

Reading the enigmatic Laurance Rockefeller is especially difficult. Wrote family biographers Peter Collier and David Horowitz: "As one straddling the fence between business and the environment, he knew he could be an effective salesman of the concept of conservationist concern, allaying the fears of industrial leaders that the push for protection masked an antibusiness attitude." Often pushed by his dig-we-must brother Nelson, he saw "no inconsistency," the authors continued. Conservation was just one side of the equation; the other was jobs, growth, development, and profit. "He was very much a background figure in a group photograph," the biographers write.

> Compared to the other starkly defined people, he seemed slightly out of focus, his motion not quite frozen by the camera's shutter. When he was captured, it was not looking ahead full face, but glancing over his brother's shoulder at someone else in the group, the habitual look of detached amusement on his face.

Despite the reluctance of the senior Rockefellers, the Storm King outcome encouraged a new spirit among many other regional leaders.

Much diminished in their importance are the faded icons of the old Hudson economy: the gray-suited managers from General Electric, General Motors, and IBM. To replace them the Duggans and Stowells were joined by many citizens who pitched in with fresh ideas. Wall Street lawyers Samuel Pryor and William Evarts, brother-in-law of an early head of the Nature Conservancy, were among these. Another was the fiery Yale Art School graduate Franny Reese, a beloved mainstay on the Con Edison battleground who later served for many years as Scenic Hudson's chair and remained active until her death in a car accident at age eighty-five. The recently deceased attorney Constantine Sidamon-Eristoff was indefatigable, as are his widow and sister, both named Anne. Top corporate lawyer Frederic Rich became Scenic Hudson's chair. Christopher J. ("Kim") Elliman was lured away from a comfortable investment management position to become CEO of the Open Space Institute. Philanthropist Joan K. Davidson braved the rough and tumble of Albany politics as head of the state's parks department. So did her much-admired successor Carol Ash, who later headed a private organization dedicated to maintaining and expanding the state's already impressive network of parks and protected areas.

As part of the 1980 Hudson River Settlement, Con Edison was required to chip in twelve million dollars to establish the Manhattan-based Hudson River Foundation to conduct fishery research. Says Joan Davidson, a staunch supporter of the project, "The foundation has saved the sturgeon population in the Hudson River, keeps tabs on toxic chemicals, provides high-level monitoring of river quality, has trained a generation of river scientists, manages the collaboration of scientists and environmentalists restoring the legendary oysters of the lower Hudson River, and runs an effective program of grants for the improvement of Hudson Valley communities." For many years the foundation has been ably led by philanthropist Ned Ames and attorney Clay Hiles.

Lawyer John Adams, who, having grown up on a farm in the Catskills, was central in the early development of Scenic Hudson, later became a founder of the Open Space Institute and (along with Stephen Duggan) of the now prominent Natural Resources Defense Council with its global footprint. In 2011 the scrappy Adams, who disguises his competitive spirit behind a mild manner while enjoying hyperactive retirement, was a popular choice to win the Medal of Freedom, the highest honor a US president can bestow upon a civilian. The business-minded Ned Sullivan has guided the development of Scenic Hudson with great energy and skill. Historical-house enthusiast J. Winthrop Aldrich has devoted decades to the task of achieving new definitions of "highest and best use" for the valley's precious old dwellings, lands, and landscapes. Also in the fray have been William Schuster at the Black Rock Forest Consortium, gifted specialists at the Open Space Institute, and myriad increasingly effective local land trusts.

Some leaders in the valley, while not environmentalists, have in one sense or another made notable contributions to the gathering strength of the green economy. Among them are Leon Botstein, the energetic president of Bard College, and his counterparts at nearby Marist and Vassar Colleges; Peter Stern, and his son John and daughters Beatrice and Lisa; and director and curator David Collens of the Storm King Art Center; former director Michael Govan and his replacement Susan Sayre Batton at the art museum Dia:Beacon; and lawyer Judith LaBelle of Glynwood Center, a group dedicated to saving family farming in the valley.

The affable David Redden, vice chairman of Sotheby's auction house in New York and a Cornwall weekender, manifests the new energy. Taxed with a demanding day job, he has also served on myriad non-profit boards in the valley, including a six-year stint as Scenic Hudson's chairman, and has done much to keep environmentally sensitive politicians such as Congressman Maurice Hinchey in office. "It's amazing,"

Redden says. "Just look around and think of one place or another. These groups have all been remarkably successful at what they do, and they've become incredibly good at fund-raising. And that, of course, is the key. Unless you have money, all you can do is dream."

And at least until the Great Recession struck in 2008, there was a consistent flow of new money to fuel the dreams. By far the biggest chunk of it that has flowed into Hudson conservation in recent years has come from a bountiful and strangely unlikely private source: DeWitt and Lila Acheson Wallace, the founders of the prodigiously successful *Reader's Digest* magazine empire and reigning monarchs presiding over the vast income it generated. The sordid story of bitter court intrigue, savage office politics, blatant thievery, and general depravity, especially during the later years, when both Wallaces aged and became increasingly unable to think clearly, has been fully told elsewhere. But it's worth taking a quick look at the odd course of events that ended up endowing the Hudson Valley so vastly.

At the outset in the 1920s, when the Wallaces worked diligently in a little apartment above a garage, it was difficult to foresee that their offerings of condensed material from other publications would find such an immense global public. My mother, no intellectual but an avid reader who wanted to keep up on things, never failed to have a stack of *Reader's Digest* condensed books on her bedside table. She and millions of others devoured those books. As the company's revenues swelled and money started pouring in during the 1930s, the Wallaces held on to all voting stock of the private parent company, the Reader's Digest Association. Over the years the value of these shares increased as profits soared, but it was difficult to come up with precise figures since no market had been made.

Lila Wallace had long been interested in gardens and stately houses, starting with the opulent High Winds property in Mount Kisco, Westchester County, where the couple lived in great style. In 1958 she paid lavishly to buy a beautiful stretch of river-view land in Garrison and replant there a federal-style mansion called Boscobel. Originally located fifteen miles downriver, the house had been torn apart, its pieces stored in barns and stables at various sites, to make way for a hospital. The property was trucked piecemeal to the new site and beautifully reassembled there. Surrounded by bountiful gardens, the house and grounds became a popular attraction, with magnificent river views and a lively program of events (spike heels not allowed, nor more than two children per family in tour groups).

The place went through a bad patch, reported John Heidenry in his exhaustive book *Theirs Was the Kingdom* about the Wallace saga, thanks to the tastes of William Kennedy, the decorator assigned to the interior of the house. "Boscobel had been an elegant example of the Federal period," Heidenry wrote, "but for Kennedy the main thing was to fill up the house with rare, expensive, and beautiful things just so long as they were American and roughly from the early nineteenth century, give or take a hundred years." Kennedy was also eventually found guilty of putting fake art into the mansion, stealing millions from the Wallaces via purchases of furniture through a dummy company that he controlled, and other major transgressions. When found out, he was eventually banished from the "kingdom" and the interior re-redecorated with authentic furnishings. Some are reproductions, but, says Geoffrey Platt Jr., former executive director, visitors seem not to mind.

In 1938 the Wallaces had created a Reader's Digest Foundation to which, from time to time, they donated stock. But the vastly greater share of their philanthropy, especially as practiced later in their lives, involved the establishment of a series of "support organizations" that would receive Reader's Digest stock allocations. The first of these, founded in 1980 when DeWitt Wallace was close to death, benefitted Macalester College in Minnesota, an institution with which Wallace had long been involved. But later six other "support organizations" to benefit prominent institutions of special interest to Laurance Rockefeller and to the Wallaces' lawyer, Barnabas McHenry, but not necessarily of particular interest to either Wallace, also came into being. Colonial Williamsburg, the Metropolitan Museum of Art, and the Bronx Zoo were among the recipients of this largesse.

Another "support organization," which appeared to come out of nowhere, was called the Fund for Hudson Highlands. It was given a mandate to preserve land in the Hudson Highlands region where Boscobel is located. For years the Wallaces had made generous annual donations to Scenic Hudson and the Open Space Institute. In 2001, after both Wallaces had died, the Fund for Hudson Highlands was liquidated. After a bitter struggle between competing conservation groups, all its assets, eventually valued at $422 million, were split evenly between Scenic Hudson and OSI.

Creative use of these endowments had involved establishing conservation easements, transfers, and purchases of development rights. There have been many deals with other private and public donors, as well as straightforward acquisitions of land. Often successful efforts to generate matching funds from public sources have done much to stretch those Wallace dollars and keep the capital intact. At last count OSI said it had protected more than one hundred thousand acres in New York State, in large part with Wallace funds. Scenic Hudson, which claims twenty-five thousand protected acres, has embarked on a major effort to sequester an additional sixty-five thousand acres of "the land that matters most." Viewsheds, watersheds, and ridgelines get special attention.

Often the Wallace beneficiary organizations display ingenuity in preserving corridors of open space for wildlife or hikers or to inhibit sprawl. Ned Sullivan of Scenic Hudson showed me an example: a pretty wooded pathway between Franklin D. Roosevelt's Springwood residence at Hyde

Park and Eleanor Roosevelt's nearby Val-Kill retreat that the organization bought to prevent this land's surrender to further sprawl along busy Route 9 north of Poughkeepsie.

⚫

The hamlet of Garrison in Putnam County, which falls within the town of Philipstown, offers an example of how tight a grip—too tight, some feel—private conservationists have won on valuable land in many parts of the valley. In these parts, tucked away in the eastern folds of the Hudson Highlands, growing swarms of weekenders and full-time residents, not a few with famous boldface names, live hidden behind trees and walls in a rich assortment of converted barns, castles, hunting lodges, regular houses designed by illustrious architects, and the occasional McMansion. The community is bracketed by two sadly overrun towns, Fishkill on one flank and Peekskill on the other. Many of Garrison's old families, especially the Osborns and the Perkinses, have worked hard, with the Hudson Highlands Land Trust and the Open Space Institute as allies, to preserve the landscapes into which such places are built. The owners wanted more to see the views than to be seen. They gobbled up the land in big parcels, then handed it over to nonprofit charities with tight strings attached. Philanthropist Chris Davis bought the beautifully situated but floundering Garrison Golf Club, in large measure out of a desire to prevent three hundred town houses from being built on the site. Today, driving northward from the Bear Mountain Bridge on the two-lane Highway 9D, you'd hardly know you were in a village but for a couple of blinking yellow lights; a filling station; a post office; a casually run cafe where you can get the newspaper and a cup of coffee when the proprietors feel like opening up; a handsome library; and, craning your neck, the Episcopal church I attended as a child. In Philipstown, wrote Peter Boyer in the *New Yorker:*

Activist groups in the triumphant coalition evolved into a network of foundations with powerful influence in the Highlands, advocating against development and acquiring vast tracts of private land, much of it from Gilded Age estates, for conversion into open-space preserves. In a real sense, preservation became the new local industry.

Boyer's article, as well as a profile in *Esquire,* describe the arrival in the area of Fox News chairman Roger Ailes as a weekend resident; his 2008 purchase of a local weekly, the *Putnam County News and Recorder (PCN&R);* and the installation of his wife Beth as its publisher. At the time the final steps were being taken toward full approval of a new zoning plan for Philipstown that upholds basic environmental values, reducing density at full build-out and protecting from unsightly development some of the wooded ridgelines that do much to give the town its special character. To the dismay of many in the community, Ailes's paper began railing against property taxes and against some of the zoning restrictions then under consideration and arguing that the preservationists' actions were not for the "greater good," as they often claimed. Ailes also flexed a strong arm at public hearings, causing at least some local officials to feel threatened by possible lawsuits, and warning of sharp reactions to visits to his property by environmental officials.

Eventually, some of Ailes's recommendations found their way into the new, one-hundred-page zoning plan. *PCN&R's* editor Joseph Lindsley, installed by Ailes in 2009, told Boyer that "in the end the town supervisor, the Land Trust, and all the people who have been advocating for the zoning acknowledge that all the changes have been good." The widely admired Andrew Chmar, a retired army colonel who runs the land trust, agrees. But he puts a different spin on the outcome. He says that many of the improvements came because of the local business community's effective participation, not as a result of hectoring by Ailes.

At the end of the day, Chmar says, Ailes seemed to be arguing less for the public good than for self-serving reasons having to do with possible zoning restrictions on his own property. Ironically, Chmar observes, "He moved here precisely because of what he's now opposing."

"Ailes would love to say that it's just an elitist thing, that it's all just the rich people up on the hill, but he's completely wrong," says one longtime resident. "All kinds of people want to preserve the place."

In many respects then, late in the twentieth century and early in the twenty-first, private leaders and institutions played major roles in sparing the region from the pollution, sprawl, and heedless surrender of open space that had so badly disfigured other parts of the region, such as western Long Island and much of New Jersey. Around the Hudson one finds new determination not to allow more land, especially working farmland, to give way to conventional development. Ground has been gained on tackling pollution by means of countless legal maneuvers. Strikingly, the mainsprings of the valley's revival extend far beyond the efforts of environmentalists, community activists, a handful of caring lawmakers, and the other usual suspects.

As the new century began, many broader forces were also pointing toward the affinities between environmental protection and restoration and economic and cultural revival. For all that has been accomplished, less than 2 percent of New York State's private land is protected. Biological resources continue to be squandered. Much hard work lies ahead. But thankfully, the spirit of Dr. Partridge is once again abroad in the land.

CHAPTER 4

On the Offensive

A PRIME EXAMPLE OF HOW THE STORM KING BATTLE PUT CONSERVA-tionists on the offensive comes from Black Rock Forest, a beautiful 3,830-acre tract of forest, streams, ponds, and former farmland on Storm King Mountain's western slope. Black Rock Forest's topography is "precipitous," wrote environmental historian Neil Maher. Nineteenth-century families owning land there struggled to make a living from multicrop farming and logging. Much later it seemed likely that this parcel of open space, which had come into Harvard University's hands, would fall victim to checkerboard development.

Those prospectively affected did not remain indifferent. Rather, they thronged to the task of saving the forest, and with the help of an imaginative and generous deus ex machina, they came up with a creative solution. Now governed by a nonprofit consortium, the forest functions not as a housing subdivision but as a vibrant research and recreation facility. The forest's lands remain intact, carefully studied and well used and spared from the kinds of pollution that would have arrived along with conventional development.

The story begins in 1885, when New York banker James Stillman moved to Cornwall, where he had attended boarding school. He aspired to join the blue-chip gated community of Tuxedo Park located nearby. But he had been blackballed on the grounds that his richesse was too nouveau to suit grandees such as Tuxedo's founder, tobacco magnate Pierre Lorillard Jr. The rebuffed Stillman then sought to establish a large part of Black Rock Forest as his own Tuxedo Park replica—an exclusive compound for family and friends. First he bought a big spread on Storm King Mountain for his own family's use. Then, over two decades, he acquired a series of adjacent holdings. But his development scheme never worked. When he died in 1918, his son, Dr. Ernest Stillman, inherited the property in what Neil Maher called a "ruinous state," cut over for use as fuel for brick kilns and foundries.

The Harvard-educated Ernest Stillman was much taken by the work and thoughts of Gifford Pinchot, the first chief of the US Forest Service under President Grover Cleveland. Pinchot harbored ideas about "scientific forestry," calling for the nation's woodlands to be protected and renewed for human benefit. The concept was scorned by John Muir and other purists who passionately believed in leaving wilderness alone in such places as California's Hetch Hetchy River near Yosemite, where damming threatened. Abandoning his father's idea of founding a new Tuxedo Park, Ernest Stillman in 1928 set about to establish Black Rock Forest as a testing ground for silviculture experiments and, following the Pinchot model, for the "wise use" of its trees as fuel. Though the property could not be considered "virgin," it contained a profusion of wildlife and vegetation, including more than twenty plant species classified as rare.

The data collected over a long period, starting in the 1930s, from a site so close to New York City remains useful to scientists. According to the *New Yorker* writer George W. S. Trow, whose June 11, 1984, "Annals of Discourse" piece remains a classic work about the forest, Dr. Stillman wanted this land to be "constantly useful and also constantly flourishing." His forester Hal Tryon and a small crew did much to restore and improve the property. Detailed records were kept.

Dr. Stillman died in 1949 and, along with a $1.2 million endowment, left the forest to Harvard with the understanding (but no formal commitment) that scientific work would continue there. Harvard never said it would use the forest, only that it would maintain it. But although a few good scientific papers came out of the years of Harvard ownership as a result of occasional increments of research, the university employed only one full-time person to manage the place. It preferred to use the Harvard Forest in Petersham, Massachusetts, much closer to Cambridge, for forestry research.

Harvard did allow public access to the forest's roads and trails, conceding fishing rights and a deer-hunting season to members of the Black Rock Fish and Game Club in return for security patrols. Not watching closely, the university gave other visitors excellent opportunities for hiking, snowmobiling, cross-country skiing, ice skating, and swimming in Sutherland Pond, the only one of the forest's ponds that does not drain into Cornwall's drinking water system. In other respects Harvard neglected the property. "We have made virtually no use of Black Rock," admitted Harvard's general counsel, Daniel Steiner, in 1981, "but it is burdened by substantial maintenance costs."

During this period nearby residents, including Stephen and Smokey Duggan, Esty and Hellie Stowell, and others who had been active in the Con Edison warfare, became apprehensive about the fate of the forest. The power company's pumped storage facility would have inundated four hundred acres of land within the forest and blocked use of the sole open-access road. Even so, a three-member committee appointed by Harvard president Derek Bok recommended that the university take no position on the Con Edison proposal. While the committee also stated its view that Harvard should not sell the land for small-lot development, suspicions were mounting that this in fact was under consideration. Steiner told Trow that Harvard had "no intention of disposing of the forest for development." He did admit that "alternative ownership" was in mind.

It was also clear that Harvard planned to hold on to the proceeds of any sale, as well as the Stillman endowment, which despite outlays for maintenance had, Trow reported, grown in worth to $2,490,964 by 1983. Esty Stowell, a 1934 Harvard graduate, launched a correspondence with Steiner. What he got back, he told Trow, was "in most instances a total mouthful of feathers." An infuriated John Stillman, Dr. Stillman's son and an energetic conservationist who had vigorously opposed the expansion of the nearby Stewart Field into New York's fourth jetport, threatened to sue, even though Harvard felt that its legal position was secure.

With matters remaining at an impasse, Steiner in 1981 sought advice from a family friend, investment banker, science policy advocate, and philanthropist William T. Golden, then also the board chair at New York City's American Museum of Natural History. "I know of your interests in forests, Bill," said Steiner, "and of your involvement in the Catskills, and that you have hiked in Black Rock. What do you think we should do?" The imaginative Golden, who died in 2007 at age ninety-seven after a remarkable life, favored an option that was one of several that Harvard's committee had proposed: form a consortium of about a dozen city-bound institutions to buy the forest and use it for "research, education, and relaxation."

Steiner uncovered enthusiasm, especially among universities and private schools. Eventually, Golden, known for his willingness to "buy the first tank of gas" to get a worthy project started, acquired the forest for four hundred thousand dollars in 1989. He put it into "the not-for-profit Black Rock Forest Preserve, which in turn leases the Forest to the not-for-profit Black Rock Forest Consortium," he said. "Harvard then contributed the purchase price as an endowment for the Forest, to which I also contributed." Harvard did, however, hang on to the Stillman family's endowment.

One of the consortium board's early acts was to advertise for a new executive director. Selected was forester William Schuster, a young Columbia University graduate with skills in management and fundraising, as well as in his field of forestry. He arrived on-site in 1992 and soon concluded that for the consortium to work the forest would need overnight lodging facilities. "Black Rock will make your school a better place," Schuster began telling prospective consortium members. Over the years he and his board generated $4.2 million in capital funds, chiefly from the Kresge Foundation, Columbia University, and the National Science Foundation, and have constructed an excellent physical plant with a sixty-bunk dormitory building and a second, smaller building with office space, classrooms, and labs.

These buildings boast award-winning green features, including geothermal heating and cooling, solar panels, and other such amenities. After a slow start during the early years, the buildings and grounds now hum with activity. All twenty consortium members are actively engaged, averaging ten trips per school per year. Every local student visits the forest at least once, and it has become very popular in the community. The annual operating budget has risen from $120,000 to about $1 million. The full-time staff has grown from one to seven. Seventy-two science projects are underway. Several researchers from the American Museum of Natural History are working there at any given time. "Science is showing us the specific ways in which our forest is responding to climate change," says Schuster. "Three tree species once here have gone, and seven new ones have come in, and doubtless we'll see more of this."

The consortium's twentieth anniversary celebration in 2010 took place, appropriately, at New York City's Century Association, venue for many prior gatherings to discuss "saving" the Hudson Valley's forests and open space in the region. A time line prepared for the event shows how the young institution has blossomed and developed. In 1992 consortium scientists discovered a new species of plankton. In 1996 it welcomed its twenty-five thousandth visitor; the fifty thousandth arrived in 1999, the hundred thousandth in 2005. In 2004 a meteorological station giving scientists access to remote data was added, and native eastern brook trout have been restored to forest streams. In 2009 the five hundredth research publication was produced, and investigation continued on the multiple impacts of oak losses within the forest.

On it goes, with the forest scoring success after success with regard to science and meeting education, recreation, and conference needs at every level from local community to international. Harvard's duplicity had generated not just anger but action on the part of environmental leaders. While Cornwall suffers from not having the forest's acres on the tax rolls, the community has gained a major educational and recreational resource that comes virtually free of charge.

<hr />

The sometimes nasty struggle over Black Rock Forest centered on the desirability of preserving open space for science and recreation and access for the general public as well as for consortium members. The subsequent, far larger, and far more complex effort to save Sterling Forest in southern Orange County was built around gathering opposition to the threat of sprawl, and resulting pollution, in an area of critical importance. This twenty-thousand-acre tract, while small in contrast to the great wilderness areas of the western United States where he had previously worked is, said former Palisades Interstate Park executive director Robert Binnewies, "the last great, single-owner tract within sight of New York City's skyscrapers." Its rocky, hilly, pond-studded landscape provides habitat for many notable wildlife species, including black bears, bobcats, coyotes, timber rattlers, many large birds, and native trout. Although humans had for many years built ironworks to exploit the region for its rich iron ore deposits, few people had actually lived in the beautiful but hardscrabble tract known as Sterling Forest. If not "pristine," this land so close to the huge metropolis remains almost miraculously unbroken.

In 1866 the railroad tycoon Edward H. Harriman, already a land-holder of vast acreage in the region, completed the purchase of the forest from its previous owner, the Sterling Iron and Railway Company. "Through control of the company," wrote Binnewies, "Harriman could look west and east from Arden House, the baronial mansion that he had built high on a ridge line of the vast estate, and see almost nothing but his own land stretching to the horizon." Offered the parcel as a gift during the Great Depression, New York State's Palisades Interstate Park Commission (PIPC) declined on the grounds that it lacked the resources to manage the land. After many subsequent years of unsuccessful tinkering in Albany with the question of how to incorporate the tract into the Palisades Interstate Park, reported the late community-based activist Ann Botshon in her book *Saving Sterling Forest,* 18,500 acres of this prized land were sold in 1954 to City Investing Company, a private real estate firm in New York, for under one million dollars.

City Investing, wrote Botshon, did not put those dollars on the table "in order to quietly contemplate the magnificent vistas and the rich flora and fauna or to make life good for a handful of hikers." According to a *New York Times* report, the company initially envisioned an "enormous community" of four hundred thousand to five hundred thousand people and supporting services. Provisions were made for a "totally planned scientific and educational campus," a sort of "corporate park and university think tank," as one observer put it— an "industrial Utopia" to be linked to the rest of the world by a new exit from the nearby New York State Thruway. Later, consultants told the company that much of the forest was too steep or rocky for conventional subdivision. "This land simply cannot be developed," says veteran Sterling Forest watcher Jurgen Wekerle. Accordingly, the figures began to scale down. Subsequent plans advanced by the Sterling Forest Corporation, as the operating arm of a succession of corporate owners was known, reduced the number of residents to be expected (14,500 in a 1991 version of the development plan). But high-density development and severe forest fragmentation remained principal features of the company's proposal.

Advocates of the project advanced familiar arguments in its favor. Construction jobs would materialize. Local communities would gain new tax revenues plus amenities—playgrounds, swimming pool, ball fields—that the company promised and that appealed to some local officials. Since the forest was not pristine wilderness but an area that had once been industrialized, backers of the development proposal claimed it to be consistent with historical forms of land use. Vigorous environmental stewardship was solemnly pledged. Speculators who had purchased adjacent land, expecting that development of the forestland would increase its value, expressed support.

But the more the neighboring communities of Warwick and Tuxedo heard about the proposal, the less most residents liked it. Apprehension mounted about multiple issues ranging from threats to drinking water to traffic congestion to storm-water management and sewage disposal. Environmental groups argued that the proposed development would cost local taxpayers far more to provide services for the new communities—police, fire protection, schools, highway maintenance—than they would gain in tax revenues. For every new dollar brought in, according to one study, the cost of these services would be $1.36. There was a mounting sense of the scenic and even spiritual importance of this landscape, with the thoughts and writings of the Hudson Valley's romantic artists and writers reverberating on its cherished hillsides.

The company had long made it clear that it was prepared either to sell the forest or develop it, whichever would be the more lucrative. With development plans still on hold as of the early 1980s, and no funding available anywhere for a buyout, a grassroots movement was launched in the mid-1980s with the twin goals of blocking development efforts and generating financial support from multiple federal, state, and private sources. Leading the movement was a young couple, Paul and JoAnn Dolan, New York City dwellers who had a weekend house near the forest and used it for hiking and recreation. When energetic media efforts and endless meetings failed to achieve results beyond consciousness raising, forest preservation advocates launched a new organization, the Sterling Forest Liaison Committee (later the Sterling Forest Coalition [SFC]), to extend the opposition's reach and draw in powerful outsiders with influential contacts. Brought in to lead this charge was Pace University law professor John Humbach, a property law expert with passionately held concerns about preventing partially treated sewage flowing out of the wounded forest from fouling drinking water supplies for millions of users beyond the forest's boundaries.

Humbach's vigorous efforts kindled moral support for the opposition to the company's scheme. So did those of another high-voltage advocacy group, Sterling Forest Resources, charged with mobilizing grassroots support. But as the company's asking price shot up to two hundred million dollars or more, funds available for even a partial purchase remained at nil. So an even more power-laden group was formed in 1993. Named the Public-Private Partnership to Save Sterling Forest (PPP), it was chaired by Larry Rockefeller of the Natural Resources Defense Council. Private sector members included representatives of the Environmental Defense Fund, the Appalachian

Mountain Club, the Nature Conservancy, the Trust for Public Land and Barnabas McHenry (representing DeWitt and Lila Acheson Wallace and their Reader's Digest fortune), Scenic Hudson, and the Open Space Institute.

From the public sector came members of key New York State agencies, including the Palisades Interstate Park Commission, the Hudson River Greenway Council, and the North Jersey District Water Supply Commission. An adjunct group in Washington comprised Congressional staff members. Included were assistants to then US representative Peter Kostmayer (D-PA), who in 1990 had "put Sterling Forest on the federal radar," said Ann Botshon, by launching the very first bill calling for funds to buy it. PIPC's Robert Binnewies became the group's "taskmaster," charged with coordinating PPP's efforts in fund-raising, public education, and involvement in the Environmental Impact Statement process.

For the next three years there ensued a dizzying sequence of political moves at the state and federal level. In New Jersey, Governor Christine Todd Whitman pledged to provide support, but not until New York chipped in; for a long time, until Governor Mario Cuomo managed to obtain passage of a law creating a new Environmental Protection Fund, New York said it had no money. Federal House and Senate bills put forward in 1994 faltered as a result of a surprise dissent from the National Park Service and failed to make the cut at the hectic end of that summer's legislative session. Later, though House Speaker Newt Gingrich became a surprise advocate for preserving Sterling Forest, various bills suffered when special-interest legislators conditioned their support on the inclusion of quid pro quo funding for pet projects elsewhere. Suggested trade-offs included selling four million acres of Oklahoma grasslands to buy the forest, yielding thousands of acres of wilderness in Utah for the 2002 Winter Olympics, and extending for two years the opportunity for the Ketchikan Pulp Company to buy timber from Alaska's treasured Tongass National Forest.

But finally, in 1996–97, after years of patient spadework by New York representatives Maurice Hinchey, Marge Roukema, and Ben Gilman; New Jersey congressman (later senator) Bob Torricelli and senators Bill Bradley and Frank Lautenberg; others on Capitol Hill; and Governor George Pataki in Albany, a funding package at last began to come together. New sources of funds included President Bill Clinton's Omnibus Parks and Public Lands Management Act of 1996 and revenues from New York State's $1.75 billion Clean Water–Clean Air Bond Act, which won public approval in the election that year. Meanwhile, representatives of the Open Space Institute and of the Trust for Public Land were meeting in secret with SFC's CEO Louis Heimbach to hammer out the outlines of a contract that would transfer to PIPC all but a small portion of the forest. What resulted was a deal announced in February 1997 in which, for $55 million, the buyers would get 15,280 acres of the forest, leaving 2,220 remaining acres for the company to own and perhaps develop.

The ensuing contract called for a down payment, which was supplied from the Lila Acheson and DeWitt Wallace Fund for the Hudson Highlands. Other increments included $10 million from New Jersey, a total of $16 million from New York, and $17.5 million in federal funds; $1.5 million came from miscellaneous sources, including a benefit bicycle ride from Seattle to Bear Mountain that was undertaken by four college students. To cap the deal a final $5 million came from the Doris Duke Charitable Trust.

For those who uncompromisingly wanted all 17,500 acres or nothing, it was a letdown. But Pataki and Whitman both crowed at a February 1998 ceremony to celebrate the deal. The activist Paul Dolan called it "a unique example of vision from the bottom up." Binnewies wrote that his involvement reached "a level of intensity that would personally challenge my endurance like nothing I had ever encountered in my professional career, or could ever have imagined." But he continued, the standing forest, now an important part of New York's state park system, is "a living monument to the conservation ethic." Added Ann Botshon: "In working to save Sterling Forest, and to preserve the highlands beyond, environmentalists are attempting to return to the early twentieth-century vision that believed in strong action on behalf of the public good."

The story has an epilogue. The 1997 agreement creating what would become Sterling Forest State Park had exempted almost all of it from development. By the early 2000s an additional twenty-three million dollars had been spent on expanding the park via public purchases of additional woodlands in the area. Still, Sterling Forest LLC (as the Sterling Forest Corporation was renamed in a corporate reorganization) did not abandon its efforts to salvage some profit from the wreckage of its plans. The company's most controversial proposal was to convert the last property it owned, a 571-acre inholding within the forest, which became known as the "hole in the doughnut," into a luxury golf course and 107-mansion residential development. Massive restructuring of the landscape and forest fragmentation were planned "to allow for a perfect tee shot," as veteran critic Jurgen Wekerle put it.

Community feelings once again ran strong. Some local officials, as usual, favored the project as a source of jobs and property taxes. But much of the land now in play was an old iron mine that had been in heavy use during the Revolutionary War, and opposition mounted for reasons principally having to do with watershed protection and threats from extensive bedrock blasting. The influential New York–New Jersey Trail Conference complained lustily that the blasting, plus the use of heavily metal-laden water and chemicals on the golf course, would threaten the integrity of drinking water for two million people in New

York and New Jersey who depend on the Ramapo and Wanaque reservoir systems.

Many of those citizens who had led the long previous battle once again mounted the barricades. Once again, they got help from Albany. First, the state's Department of Environmental Protection verified that a substantial portion of the site designated for the golf course was important habitat for timber rattlesnakes and ruled it should remain undisturbed. Subsequently, the company abandoned the golf course proposal. Then in 2004 it dropped the entire idea. In 2006 an agreement was reached for New York State to buy the whole tract for $13.5 million, once again drawing funds from the state's Environmental Protection Fund. The transaction, said a beaming Governor Pataki, "represents the final step in protecting the full array of natural resources and wildlife habitats at Sterling Forest State Park for generations to come."

Now the emboldened environmentalists took aim at an even bigger target: natural resource protection for watershed land in the 3.5-million-acre Eastern Appalachian belt called the Highlands. This crescent-shaped band of land, much of it adjacent to densely populated areas from Pennsylvania to New Jersey, New York, and northwest Connecticut, also provides drinking water, via eighteen hundred miles of streams, for more than ten million people. The area had long suffered from heavy development pressure, with five thousand acres a year falling to the bulldozer's blade at the height of the real estate bubble early in the twenty-first century. For years politicians in all four states, but especially in New Jersey, faced tremendous pressures from developers and local municipalities and counties to allow sprawl to invade more and more of the watershed. For years opposing forces struggled without success to muster votes for better management.

In 2004 the logjam was at last broken, thanks in part to a major summer drought that jeopardized water supplies in much of the region.

In New Jersey legislators passed the Highlands Water Protection and Planning Act, which placed strict controls over development within an eight-hundred-thousand-acre band of land in the state's northwestern portion. In the most environmentally sensitive sections, construction would be forbidden within three hundred feet of any open water. Elsewhere, limited development would be tolerated, but standards would be set by a governing board. Other provisions included funding for land acquisition, transfer of development rights, reimbursement to selling landowners for reductions in state assessed property values, and real estate tax breaks. Help to local communities included authorization to charge fees and provide assistance from the state attorney general in the event of lawsuits from developers. Jeff Tittel, head of New Jersey's Sierra Club chapter, crowed that the bill's passage marked "D-Day in the war on sprawl."

In Washington in November 2004, after an aggressive campaign and what the Environmental Defense Fund called "unprecedented collaboration" among congresspeople of both parties from all four states, both houses passed and President George W. Bush signed the supportive Highlands Conservation Act. Getting it done involved taming some of the most ferociously antienvironmental private property rights zealots around. One was the flamboyant former Northern California representative Richard Pombo, who had to be cajoled to get the Highlands bill released from his committee and placed on the House floor for action by the full membership. At one key moment in this struggle, it seemed likely that Pombo would keep the bill bottled up within the Natural Resources subcommittee, which he then headed. But novice congresswoman Sue Kelly of New York's Westchester County stressed to Pombo that the bill contained no provisions for "takings," anathema to many property rights proponents, and that it would not weaken local jurisdictions' power in their land dealings with state and federal agencies. Won over, Pombo expressed love for the bill, loudly stating that it constituted model land-use legislation. It sailed out of committee and soon became law.

No sooner had the ink dried on these laws, and implementation seriously began in 2007, than opponents began to chisel away at them. Despite vigorous efforts from elected officials in all four Highlands states, the US Congress only managed to cough up an initial appropriation of two million dollars versus the authorized ten million. Many seats on the Highlands Council mandated under the state law remained unfilled, and in many other respects, said Tittel, the plan suffered from "lack of implementation." And in 2009, with recession under way and a tightfisted Republican governor, Chris Christie, newly installed in office, it only got worse. Highlands funding was cut to barely more than one-third of its previous level, and other funding cuts were so severe that, warned Tittel, there were "concerns that implementation of the Highlands Act will stall and eventually be dismantled."

Some expressed relief. The New Jersey act, said columnist Paul Mulshine in the Bergen *Star-Ledger*, was "an idea whose time has gone." In troubled economic times, he argued, it would be better to increase residential development opportunities rather than reduce them. "Back in 2004," he wrote, "the deep thinkers of both parties were seduced by the notion that economic growth in the state was so strong that we could afford to put some of the most desirable real estate on the planet off-limits to development for eternity." Using arguments as outmoded as he claimed the Highlands legislation's proponents' were, he went on to applaud Christie's stated intent to "restore economic development" in the Highlands.

Now, though, any such move would be hotly contested by the energetic Highlands Coalition, a four-state organization listing as members a diverse group of 180 private and public organizations dedicated to the idea of keeping the Highlands flame alive. It aggressively lobbies both in Washington and in state capitals, and with the need for water-quality protection as its principal and compelling argument, its chances of staving off the worst are good. The coalition had been deeply involved in the 2004 struggles in Washington and in Trenton. Now, once again, many of those who waged the previous battles remain engaged, and today they know the ropes better.

Both the Black Rock Forest and the several Highlands victories signal an important departure from the dominance of sprawl. For decades after World War II, the buildup of demand for affordable housing kept control of how to do it largely in the hands of developers, chief among them *Time* magazine cover boy Arthur Levitt of Levittown fame. The developers bought old farms and forestlands, clear-cut them with no respect for the natural folds and bends in the terrain, and pressed buyers to install septic tanks with limited lifetimes rather than build community sewer systems. Storm-water management and watershed protection measures were neglected. Local jurisdictions became wrongly persuaded that the new inhabitants of these communities would shell out more in property taxes than the cost of supplying them with roads, schools, police and fire protection, and other services. Shopping centers sprouted as well. So in the Hudson Valley as elsewhere, sprawl long maintained its power as a near-irresistible force, making its mark with special emphasis in areas around such communities as Albany, Poughkeepsie, Newburgh, and Peekskill.

But in the instance of Black Rock Forest, even Harvard's avaricious money managers came to see the wisdom of Bill Golden's idea that the property should be used for scientific research and the public good, rather than offer developers a chance to wall it off for the exclusive and costly use of a small number of luxury home buyers. At Sterling Forest and along the Highlands, the community activists who won the bitter fights with long-distance help from quietly influential supporters had similar arguments to advance. They also held trump cards: watershed management and the need to protect the integrity of drinking water supplies, now becoming an ever more sacred mantra in the region as human populations and densities continued their sharp rise and attacks on the landscape became ever more threatening. New antisprawl forces were on the ascent as conventional development came more and more to be seen as a form of pollution and an economic drag. Never again, as the new ethics and economic principles of prudent land use were taking shape more clearly, would developers blind to environmental considerations have an easy time of it.

Part II: The New Drivers

Chapter 5

Minding the Watershed

Aaron Burr, America's "most famous infamous man," best known for having killed former treasury secretary Alexander Hamilton in a duel in 1804, also played a poisonous role in depriving New York City's residents of adequate clean drinking water supplies. For more than three decades after his privately owned Manhattan Company was founded the same year that Hamilton succumbed to Burr's bullet, Burr and his henchmen owned exclusive rights to convey water to the city. They did precious little with those rights, preferring to invest "surplus" income in other projects and cleverly arranging a deal with the state assembly to make this possible.

The city wanted "pure and wholesome water," wrote Gerard T. Koeppel in his detailed book *Water for Gotham*. But Burr knew he had "sired a bank" that would be far more profitable from other activities than from selling water. The private company's miserable water stewardship, relying largely on polluted wells and springs within the city, directly caused Gothamites great harm from filthy streets, fires that roared out of control for lack of water to put them out, and severe supply shortages. Water-related diseases such as yellow fever and cholera attacked rich and poor alike. In the severe 1832 epidemic, cholera swept southward from Canada, killing 3,516 New Yorkers, according to the low official count.

The Manhattan Company's performance serves as strong fodder for those who regard water as a human right, not a commodity, and believe that no good can ever come from privatizing its delivery. It was also one of many missteps on water policy made during the colonial period by Dutch and British administrators. As had the island's Native Americans, Dutch settlers relied principally on spring-fed water from a deep, seventy-acre pond in Lower Manhattan east of Broadway that they called the Collect. Although this source was soon fouled by runoff from tanneries, human wastes, slaughterhouses, and other contaminants, use of the fetid pond continued well into the nineteenth century. New Yorkers also collected rainwater and purchased from street vendors expensive "tea water" from wells often fouled by privies, cesspools, and saltwater infiltration.

"New York," wrote Koeppel, "had entered the first American century with less good water than the Dutch had bequeathed the English." Even as New York became the nation's most populous city early in the 1800s, its growth was hampered by competitors with more reliable and ampler water sources, including Philadelphia and Boston. "In no way had Gotham been more foolish than in failing to procure good water," wrote Koeppel.

Once the Manhattan Company was at last dislodged from power in 1835, when voters overwhelmingly approved a measure enabling the fast-growing city's officials to import water from beyond its borders, the tide turned for good. From then to now, gifted and determined engineers and appointees have worked closely with a mixed bag of politicians to equip the staggering city with adequate amounts of clean drinking water from watersheds to the north and west. To this day New York City's water remains miraculously pure, tasty, and almost entirely free of costly filtration devices. The system, created by means of what has been called "one of the most prodigious public works projects in history," is no less than one of the world's finest. It delivers up to 1.5 billion gallons of clean water a day to more than nine million customers. Many of them remain unaware of the huge effort it took to make this happen.

"Triumph and tragedy, skill and scandal, recklessness and resolve have shared the stage on which this long-lasting drama has been played," wrote Diane Galusha in her detailed history, *Liquid Assets: A History of New York City's Water System.*

> *Careers have been built and destroyed, fortunes won and lost. Social reverberations of these massive construction projects were as profound as their imprints on the landscape, as corps of immigrant workers were recruited to cut stone or build tunnels, then stayed to leave their cultural mark on nearby communities. Politicians rode the waves of the water system's successes, or paid dearly when drought or deception resulted in water famines.*

The physical plant of what has been painstakingly pieced together, across the checkerboard of a two-thousand-square-mile watershed divided into three subwatersheds, is described and illustrated in a handsome volume called *Water-Works: The Architecture and Engineering of the New York City Water Supply.* In themselves, the photographs and detailed drawings assembled by Cooper Union researchers for this remarkable history are an art trove of impressive quality. Moreover, the mighty construction effort over three centuries constitutes a major achievement, showing how a sustained and determined effort to protect the quality of the city's drinking water has benefitted the watershed as a whole.

Early in the nineteenth century, while the city was still acutely suffering from disease outbreaks, drinking water shortages, further political maneuvers, and at least one major fire that spread widely for want of water, construction of a major new waterworks for the region at last got started. The initial source of this freshwater was the Croton watershed, which lies east and north of the Hudson and extends northward to well beyond Westchester County. Components of the system included a dam and a reservoir (Croton Lake) on the Croton River north of what later became Sing Sing prison, the 50-foot-high Croton Dam, and a thirty-three-mile aqueduct featuring the 1,450-foot High Bridge across the Harlem River.

So grand was this structure, whose centerpiece was fifteen granite arches closely resembling ancient Roman designs, that after its opening in 1848 it quickly became an attraction for tourists. Foreshadowing today's Walkway adventurers in Poughkeepsie, they enjoyed strolling along the covered viaduct (in the 1930s it was shorn of its arches and replaced by a single steel span). In 1842 freshwater from the Croton reservoir began flowing by gravity into Manhattan reservoirs, including one on the present Fifth Avenue site of the New York Public Library. Great festivities marked the aqueduct's debut on October 24 of that year. "The day began with the firing of cannons and the ringing of church bells," wrote Galusha,

> *followed by a five mile-long procession consisting of military units, politicians and nearly every civic and trade organization in the city and environs, including 4,000 firemen belonging to 52 fire companies. Temperance societies touting clean water over spirits (no liquor, only Croton water, was served at the day's events), joined butchers on horseback, scientists and clergymen who were watched by thousands of spectators . . . there were fireworks, balloon ascensions and receptions all over the city. And at City Hall, where the parade ended, the New York Sacred Music Society sang George Pope*

Morris' Croton Ode: "Water leaps as if delighted while her con-
quered foes retire! Pale contagion flies affrighted with the baffled
demon fire."

Later came periodic enlargements to the system, guiding water to
users in all boroughs but Staten Island as the city's water consumption
continued to climb. City authorities struggled to keep up, pressing on
with projects to expand the Croton system. Reservoirs blossomed. The
one originally called "Lake Manhatta" opened in 1862 and remained in
service in what is now Central Park until the 1990s. The New Croton
Aqueduct, flowing under the Harlem River beneath the High Bridge,
opened in 1890; construction had employed up to ten thousand men.

With demand steadily rising, planners' attention also moved toward
the more extensive Catskill/Delaware watershed west of the Hudson.
Once an obstructive private entity, the Ramapo Water Company, had
been forcibly dissolved by state action, city authorities moved swiftly to
bring Catskill water into town from as far as 120 miles away. It reached
the city by means of a tunnel painstakingly drilled through bedrock
1,114 feet beneath the Hudson, from Storm King Mountain on the
west to Breakneck Ridge on the east bank. About 40 percent of the city's
water now comes from the Catskills. Completed in 1927, the Catskill
system in itself was a feat involving untold thousands of workers, which
was described by author Galusha as "among the greatest engineering
accomplishments of that or any age, rivaling the Panama Canal, which
was even then being driven through the swamps of Central America."

By the 1920s, when droughts depleted the Catskill watershed
from time to time, New Yorkers cast their eyes on the even larger Delaware, whose water they shared with New Jersey and Pennsylvania.
After a US Supreme Court ruling limited the amount of water New
York could claim from the Delaware watershed to 440 million gallons

a day, work started in 1936 on the 83.8-mile Delaware Aqueduct, the world's longest continuous underground tunnel. The Delaware system, completed in 1967, encompasses about a thousand square miles, providing about half the city's water from seven reservoirs east and west of the Hudson River that can store 320 billion gallons.

Overall, the system, built over a period of 130 years, encompasses nineteen collecting reservoirs and three controlled lakes spread out over a 1,969-square-mile watershed in nine counties. Sources of this water are subwatersheds, creeks, and reservoirs whose names remain unfamiliar to most New Yorkers: Neversink and Pepacton, Schoharie and Ashokan, Esopus and Rondout. Though the Hudson supplies water for some riverside towns, including Poughkeepsie, and a facility to pump filtered Hudson River water to New York City during drought periods has long existed, it has seldom been used. About 95 percent of the city's water supply is gravity fed—a tribute to the careful work carried out by a succession of gifted engineers—and only the remaining 5 percent is electrically pumped to maintain pressures. Remarkably as well, the watershed serving most of New York City's inhabitants covers only 4.2 percent of the state's land.

Expansion of the system continues, as well as the cumbersome maintenance of what already exists. To receive and distribute water within the city, it had built two giant tunnels, one completed in 1917 and the second in 1936. Soon after, in a rare display of farsightedness, city fathers resolved to build a third huge, twenty-four-foot tunnel to act as a backup in case it became necessary to shut down one of the existing tunnels for repairs: The shutoff valves on the existing tunnels have from the outset been in continuous operation and might not reopen after having been closed. Consequences would be catastrophic, with water denied to about half the city. The backup, City Tunnel No. 3, which has been under construction since 1970, is scheduled for completion in 2020.

Another major $1.2 billion project, scheduled to get under way in 2013, is the construction of a three-mile bypass tunnel under the Hudson, from Orange to Putnam Counties. The new tunnel's purpose is to halt significant leakage from the Delaware Aqueduct's Rondout–West Branch Tunnel, which threatens city supplies and has also caused chronic flooding in two communities in the watershed, the hamlets of Wawarsing and Roseton in Ulster County. They have already experienced what Riverkeeper describes as "how the deteriorating conditions of the aqueduct can wreak havoc." A leak below the Hudson River, which the tunnel crosses at a depth of six hundred feet below the surface, is, says Riverkeeper, "an even more worrisome prospect."

In the rocky landscape of the counties north of the city, developing this intricate system was not achieved without severe hardship. Construction workers, mostly Italian and Swedish immigrants and Southern blacks arriving after the Civil War, who sometimes were allowed and even encouraged to drink whiskey on the job, faced multiple hazards. Hundreds of them were killed or mangled as a result of accidental explosions, ill-timed boom lowerings, flying rocks and other debris, floods, washouts, cave-ins, and lightning strikes. One man was impaled on a falling welding rod and after recuperating, reported Diane Galusha, returned to work only to be felled by a falling rock. An abruptly lowered derrick boom killed another. Malaria felled thousands. "Sandhogs"—specialized tunnel workers burrowing far beneath the surface—suffered from the bends. Violence was endemic. Washouts during adverse weather were frequent.

Bitter struggles between city officials and local communities persisted during the early and mid-twentieth century as the city used the power of eminent domain to seize land and evict residents. Just for the original Croton aqueduct, reported Galusha, 534 acres were taken from thirty-six landowners. In the Westchester County town of Katonah, during the construction of the New Croton Aqueduct, more than fifty houses were dragged uphill, as far as a mile, to get them up and away from a watercourse. There are countless similar stories of Catskill and Delaware communities uprooted and destroyed, vast condemnations of land, lost incomes and livelihoods. To be sure, the city compensated those owners, paid local taxes, and worked hard to treat sewage and manage storm water in the watershed. Still, complaints of inequities persist. In 2009, reported the *New York Times*, the city was receiving water from a 140-billion-gallon reservoir near a little town in the Catskills called Downsville (population 217). At the same time, public health officials were demanding that the hamlet stop tapping into this aquifer water (as they had been for a century) and spend $16,700 to cut off the springwater and run a new system off a new well. "Where's the fairness here?" asked one local politician.

The devil lived in Washington, where in 1986 Congress passed the Safe Drinking Water Act. It established that surface water-supply systems, across the board from the tiny one in Downsville to the giant in New York City, should for health reasons be equipped with expensive filtration devices. Such an installation, involving the passage of source water through fine sand to remove contaminants, would run counter to a century of the city's proud reliance on Mother Nature. Wrote the city's former Department of Environmental Protection (DEP) commissioner Albert F. Appleton in his contribution to the *Water-Works* volume: "Due to the generally pristine character of its remote watersheds and the ability of its enormous reservoir system to naturally purify the water, the city had avoided the need for filtration."

Beyond the pride, Appleton and other New York City water administrators faced a major money issue. According to city estimates, filtration if installed would cost New York ten billion to twenty billion dollars, a huge chunk of the city annual budget, plus three hundred million dollars or more in annual upkeep. Said Robert F. Kennedy Jr.: "It would have doubled water rates in the city; it would have put 250,000 people out of their homes; it would have closed down 50,000 housing units in rent controlled areas where the landlords could not pass the additional cost of the water on to their tenants." A 2008 report from the New York Public Interest Research Group (NYPIRG) alleged further practical consequences including the probable need to curtail other vital city services. And, "worst of all," NYPIRG continued, "there is no guarantee that a filtration plant will preserve public health."

The 1986 federal legislation contained a loophole allowing a waiver of the filtration mandate if, Appleton continued, "a city could demonstrate that its water had always met objective quality standards and that there was a program of watershed protection that would effectively prevent any future deterioration of water quality." The law granted communities five years to decide whether to filter or apply to the EPA for an exemption. In order to get clearance to avoid filtration, New York City in 1990 drafted onerous regulations applying to small towns in the Catskills that would set tight limits on pollution and block virtually any form of development near a watercourse.

In 1991 nine small Catskill towns banded together to fight City Hall. Over several years of sometimes harsh infighting, they worked out a billion dollar deal with the DEP to protect the watershed and also give the towns some elbow room. Buying land from willing sellers, better wastewater treatment facilities, and improved septic systems all formed part of the draft package. Concurrently, Catskill farmers banded together to form a farmer-run Watershed Agriculture Council to review watershed protection measures. It became a popular program, which Appleton called "the model for successful urban/rural partnerships and how to effectively address rural non-point source pollution." The DEP then packaged all these efforts within a draft Watershed

Memorandum of Agreement (MOA) to present to the EPA in search of a "Filtration Avoidance Determination (FAD)."

Despite all such efforts, almost everyone at the EPA believed that filtration for New York City's water would be required after the end of 1993, when a two-year extension from the city's original deadline for compliance would expire. Constantine Sidamon-Eristoff, then the EPA's Manhattan-based regional administrator, had a different view. Not granting the exemption, he felt, would lead to a surge of development in critical areas high in the watershed where a mechanical filtration system would weaken conservationists' arguments about the importance of preserving the natural filtration capacity of open space. As the staunch Republican Sidamon-Eristoff's very last day in office drew to a close in 1993, he phoned EPA administrator William K. Reilly to restate his case and ask for time to give the city a last chance. Reilly, also a Republican, conceded, ruling Democratic New York temporarily exempt from the regulation in light of the city's fervent advocacy of watershed protection. Supporting Reilly's judgment, the EPA has issued a total of five subsequent FADs. The most recent version, renewed with relatively little hostility, is good for ten years, until 2017.

Work on completing the MOA continued during this period. It had begun in 1989 when then governor George Pataki felt compelled to convene the warring factions and turn adversaries toward constructive cooperation. In 1997, culminating almost a full decade of intense debate and discussion, more than ninety stakeholders representing a wide variety of interests signed off on the thousand-page document addressed to the EPA, and it went into effect. In its final form it commits the city to spend more than $1.5 billion for watershed protection programs, including some $500 million to purchase perhaps another hundred thousand acres of ecologically sensitive watershed lands between 2007 and 2017.

The agreement enables conservation groups to negotiate easements to protect forest, agricultural lands, and wetlands in the watershed. Tough standards for waste treatment and erosion control have been set and "green" cultivation systems promoted to reduce chemical use and reduce pollutant runoff. Substantial investments to upgrade septic systems or install new ones and to improve sewage treatment plants and storm-water drains are called for. So are major outlays to settle lawsuits and for monitoring, education, and outreach, and loans and grants for economic development. Much of the management of this sprawling agenda is being done by the nonprofit Catskill Watershed Corporation, a public agency located in the town of Margaretville in the Catskills that is funded by the city and bustles with activity.

In 2008 NYPIRG and Riverkeeper, both agencies that are often critical and even scornful of the public sector's performance on environmental issues, promulgated an exhaustively researched report on how well this program is performing. The findings are remarkably positive. After examining thirty-three categories of work mandated under the 1977 MOA and the filtration avoidance determinations, the evaluation team awarded A-level grades to sixteen of them, Bs to sixteen, and Cs to only four. In its own report summarizing the first ten years of the MOA, the Catskill Watershed Corporation also awarded itself high marks: "The MOA redefined what it means to live in the watershed, to be a steward of water bound for half of the state's population. The MOA offered a bridge over troubled waters, a means of quieting the ghosts of bitter history in a quest for a mutually beneficial future. Ten years later, it is still a work in progress, but there is no denying how very much has been accomplished." Says Eric Goldstein of the Natural Resources Defense Council, who has been engaged with the region's watershed issues since the 1980s: "It's a breakthrough agreement that seems like a shotgun marriage, but one that brings material benefits to all parties. The combination of preserving water quality and filtration avoidance is a powerful device."

Currently, as a result of mounting turbidity (cloudiness) problems in water coming from fast-growing communities east of the Hudson, a new three billion dollar plant in the Bronx to filter the 10 percent of the city's water that comes from the original Croton system was scheduled to begin operating in 2012. But even in the Catskills, whose excellent water is naturally somewhat turbid, the rest of the system remains free from filtration. Wrote reporter Elizabeth Royte in the *New York Times*: "New Yorkers drink their water from Esopus Creek, from Schoharie Creek, from the Neversink River, straight from the city's many reservoirs, with only a rough screening and, for most of the year, just a shot of chlorine and chasers of fluoride, orthophosphate, and sodium hydroxide."

As ever, threats persist. One is an old chestnut that recently surfaced once again: the idea of revving up the Catskills' economy by building a giant casino there. The idea comes from a Mohican Indian group called the Stockbridge-Munsee that once lived in the Catskills, then moved to Wisconsin in the 1800s. In 2010 they were petitioning to take over 333 acres of land near the town of Thompson in Sullivan County and put there not only a 580,000-square-foot casino but also a 750-room hotel and a parking lot with 9,500 spaces that would be sited alongside the Neversink River, a famous trout stream. Backers envision that the complex would attract six million visitors a year—40 percent more than visit the Grand Canyon. New York's former governor David Paterson surprised many when in December 2010, about to leave office, he signed an agreement with the Stockbridge-Munsee band to pursue the project. Opposition was coming from many quarters, including the NRDC, which expressed watershed concerns and was calling for actions required under federal law including a "new and thorough" environmental review.

Approval of the scheme is "in the realm of when pigs fly," commented Fred LeBrun in the Albany *Times-Union*, arguing for one thing that it makes no sense for New York State to "give a franchise to print money to a Wisconsin-based tribe . . . the downside of casinos preying on the poor and those eager for a quick fix outweigh the attractions of the money spigot that beguiles the shortsighted politician."

For all the expressions of outrage on moral and practical grounds, Goldstein ranks the casino proposal as one of three principal current environmental threats to the watershed. Second of these is what he calls the "thousand cuts"—the cumulative environmental consequences of myriad smaller projects unloading new increments of nutrient or toxic pollution into the watershed. Examples would be a developer disregarding storm-water runoff; wetlands preservation regulations; or paving a large parking lot with impermeable material that greatly accelerates the flow of toxic rainwater into the watershed. Poor farmland management would also fall into this category, as would needless deforestation.

Of all current threats to the watershed, says Goldstein, the most ominous is his third issue: the fracking process now in use by companies hoping to lease Catskill land to drill for natural gas in the deep layer of northern Appalachian rock called the Marcellus Shale. The Marcellus is believed to hold the largest untapped natural gas reserve in the United States. Geologists estimate that as much as fifty trillion cubic feet of gas could be extracted from the Marcellus field, enough to supply the East Coast for fifty years. At its northeastern extremity the Marcellus overlaps with one million acres in five Catskill counties—Delaware, Schoharie, Greene, Ulster, and Sullivan—that also lie within the boundaries of New York City's watershed. The proximity of this formation to an area of heavy demand makes it all the more valuable; high prices for land leases are highly attractive to many lower-income owners of properties within the Marcellus.

The drilling method used involves mixing highly pressurized water and sand with doses of chemicals, some toxic, that help blast free the methane gas from the deep-seated rock. In fall 2010 the *Atlantic Coast-Watch* newsletter, a Sustainable Development Institute publication, published a summary of the fracking situation. Excerpts follow:

Shale drilling now accounts for about a fifth of the nation's gas production according to an MIT study, and could produce as much as 50% by 2030. An article by Christopher Bateman in Vanity Fair *magazine states that 90% of all gas wells now employ fracking.*

As described in the 2010 documentary film Gasland, *problems with this drilling process have been surfacing in Texas and the West, and those problems are now coming east. One major concern is the amount of water used—between 3 and 8 million gallons per well, according to Bateman. Of that water about 50% remains underground. The shale is deep and well below the groundwater table. There remains, however, the danger of leakage from drilling shafts and seepage upward through cracks in the rock.*

There is also the issue of what to do with tainted waste water. As of now, the water is either re-injected in the mine; or contained in open air pits on site, or trucked away to other pits—all vulnerable to leakage. The water cannot be treated by conventional wastewater treatment plants. Devon Energy, a company from Oklahoma, has developed a way to purify and reuse the water, according to the Christian Science Monitor, *but this method is costly and not required, so is not widely used. The chemical contamination of water and air surrounding the wells is causing health problems among many who have leased their land and still live in the vicinity of the wells. A barrage of complaints and suits has ensued.*

But the rush is on, and it may turn into one of the biggest energy booms in U.S. history according to CNN. The industry and others point to the advantages of producing energy from "clean" natural gas as opposed to coal fired plants, and stress that it is a domestic product that reduces U.S. dependence on foreign oil. States with depleted coffers are hungry for more revenue. States with high unemployment are desperate for the jobs these wells provide. Individual landowners who have already signed leases want to start earning their royalties. Others who have not yet signed are noticing that the value of the leases keeps ratcheting up. According to Bateman, Reliance Industries, an Indian conglomerate, recently paid Atlas Energy, a Pennsylvania firm, $1.7 billion for 120,000 acres or a whopping $14,000 an acre.

Catskills citizen Bob Keagle took a close look at fracking country in Pennsylvania in late 2010 and upon return wrote a pithy letter to a local newspaper, the *Daily Freeman.*

I recently spent several days in Wyoming County, Pa. There is a "'whole lotta fracking going on" in the beautiful Susquehanna Valley! . . .

Two years ago, when I was in Wyoming County, it was still bucolic, a throwback to times past. We were in the valley of the Susquehanna River, with rolling farmlands, hardwood forests and small town communities that dated back to pre-Revolutionary times. The river itself, beautiful and historical, meandered south to the Chesapeake Bay. Fish were in abundance, including small mouth bass and walleyed pike—prized game fish. Deer, bear, waterfowl and birds of prey, including eagles, were evident. There was peace in the valley, a great place to live and raise a family.

The change I saw when I went back was monumental. I never saw anything like it. Tens of thousands of acres had been leased by landowners to Big Gas companies. Big Gas was everywhere.

First, there were the drilling platforms. These behemoths were interspersed throughout the countryside. They were well lit at night, and could be seen for miles. The platforms were built on 15-acre pads and looked surreal, especially since they were situated in the middle of cornfields.

Then there were the trucks, sprawled all over back country roads. These were water trucks, 18-wheelers, and they operate day and night. Everywhere I went I saw them. They are employed to bring water to the abundant fracking sites. Heaven help you if you happen to get in their way on a macadam or one-lane dirt road! Heaven help the roads, as they cannot bear the traffic volume! So then the drilling companies make their own or widen existing roads, with county approval.

I wondered where the water used for fracking originates. Silly me: it comes from the Susquehanna River! There are multiple river-pumping stations and each one is allowed a million gallons of water per day, even when the river is low.

What about the ecosystems? Fish? Aquatic life? Birds? Groundwater? Insects? On and on . . . and there is no pipeline yet to bring the gas to market. Just imagine the impact of a massive pipeline to the environment when it gets going!

Ah, then there are the workers. Very few, it seems, are local. I heard a lot of Texas and southern accents. Not many residents are working on those fracking fields. The gas companies bring in their own technicians and laborers. Not much is left for the locals, save for low paying service jobs.

One thing is for certain. There is a lot of money going around. Landowners are paid anywhere from a few dollars to $7,000 or

$8,000 per acre leases. It just depends on how astute the landowner was when he or she negotiated the lease. Many of the landowners have (or had) no idea of the impact of these leases upon their land or their rural way of life.

Now some locals are waking up. They see what is going on around them. Many sense that their way of life is changing and that they made "a deal with the devil." But there is no going back. They are stuck with an ecological nightmare of epic proportions. Even now, values on the sale of leased land are plummeting. Who wants to buy land encumbered by gas company leases that will last for many years?

Could this happen in the Catskill Watershed? Do we want this kind of a nightmare in our backyard? Big Gas wants fracking in New York and money talks. We must not allow this to happen to our watersheds and our environment! Our Catskills must not suffer the same calamity as the debacle that is going on in Pennsylvania and westward.

The magnitude of both the opportunities and the hazards of Marcellus drilling can hardly be overestimated. An industry-sponsored study conducted by Penn State University pegs recoverable reserves in the entire Marcellus at "at least 489 trillion cubic feet." All New York State currently consumes natural gas at the rate of about 1.1 trillion cubic feet a year. In Pennsylvania alone, the Penn State study projects, the "Marcellus play" could be generating $13.5 billion in value added by 2020 and employing 175,000 people. Despite the obstacles, the gold rush is on, with the Catskills as a prospectively huge target if drilling there is eventually permitted.

It is hard to exaggerate the dimensions of what's at stake here. "Suddenly," says one Washington, DC–based energy expert, "We've become the world's Saudi Arabia for natural gas." But the risks are daunting. Says an apprehensive Robert Anderberg, land-use chief at the nonprofit Open Space Institute in New York City: "Fracking could kill the Catskills."

Early 2011 brought a new crop of warnings about the practice. For all the care that drillers take to manage the toxic, often radioactive water used for the drilling, including a new emphasis on recycling vast quantities of it, there are persistent risks of leakage into rivers. "Between 10 percent and 40 percent of the water injected into each well resurfaces in the first few weeks of the process," the *Times* reported, and "the wells can continue to ooze for decades after they have been hydrofracked."

Groundwater near fracking wells contained average methane gas concentrations an astonishing seventeen times higher than in nonfracking areas, according to a landmark Duke University report published by the National Academy of Sciences. The evidence of water pollution from leaky fracking came from examination of groundwater obtained from sixty-eight wells near fracking sites. The water in such places was "hopelessly polluted," said Natural Gas Watch.

Cornell University ecologist Robert Howarth issued a series of shrill warnings about the effects on the atmosphere of methane gas released by Marcellus drilling, stating that over a twenty-year cycle "shale gas is worse than conventional gas and is, in fact, worse than coal and worse than oil." The team, reported the Natural Science Foundation, had determined in a peer-reviewed paper that "extracting natural gas from the Marcellus Shale could do more to aggravate global warming than mining coal," since methane, of which "clean" natural gas is largely composed, has 105 times more "warming power" than carbon dioxide. Said Howarth: "We are not advocating for more coal or oil, but rather to move to a green, renewable future as quickly as possible. We need to look at the true environmental consequences of shale gas." "This stuff is colorless and odorless, but it could kill you," warns state assemblyman Steven Englebright, a prominent antifracking crusader.

The spring and summer of 2011 brought a rash of news from well sites that further complicates the matter. Industry claims of hydraulic fracking's safety were jarred when, on April 19, a blowout occurred at a Chesapeake Energy natural gas well in Bradford County, Pennsylvania. Some ten thousand gallons of toxic fracking fluid spewed into a nearby stream, and seven nearby homes had to be evacuated. In England experts from the British Geological Survey added earthquakes to the list of possible consequences of fracking. In two instances, reported a news blog called Independent.co.uk, earthquakes near Blackpool had occurred "at the same time that the energy company Quadrilla Resources was injecting fluids under high pressure deep underground to deliberately blast apart the gas-bearing rock." A member of the geology team said that a connection between these events was "quite likely."

Monitoring and regulatory mechanisms seem inadequate for the proper management of an industry that could experience soaring magnitude with possibly disastrous consequences for human health, property values, and the quality of life in the region. "Good luck if you want to sell your house out there," warns Englebright.

These and other recent findings were causing fracking to become ever less popular upstate, despite the prospect of quick bucks from drilling company land leases. New Yorkers polled by Marist College were almost evenly split overall. Many urban and suburbanites felt the need for reliable energy. But 47 percent of citizens living upstate, where fracking would actually occur, opposed the practice, with only 37 percent in favor. Legislators were faced with a wavering citizenry and the usual pressures, arguments, and temptations from Big Gas as well.

For all the foregoing concerns, especially over the fracking issue, most of those I talked with still feel confident about the future integrity of New York City's watershed. Galusha, for example, expresses confidence that the tide in the Catskills has turned away from the kind of development that would spell disaster for the watershed. "Local officials still feel that too much land is being taken out of development," she says, "but we're going to keep the Catskills green. This place will never be the Hamptons. This very appeal is attracting big money people. Sixty or 70 percent of the private properties around here are owned by people who don't live here but don't want sprawl." Goldstein sees an economic future for the Catskills featuring a new emphasis on tourism, local farming located close to metropolitan centers, preservation of forestlands and wetlands as natural filters on pollution, and tight storm-water management controls to protect the watershed.

So it is that avoiding the expense of filtration has become yet another major factor in the Hudson Valley's transforming economy and a public agency charged with implementing the MOA, a leading upstate transmitter of green values. "The public understands," says Tim Dillingham, a veteran of many years of fighting sprawl in the Delaware watershed. "When you rally around water with a clear message, you win."

"It's an amazing story," says Carol Ash, former head of New York State's parks department and a much-admired leader in the long struggle.

Chapter 6

The Power of Culture

William Cullen Bryant and Thomas Cole stand side by side on a broad ledge deep in the Catskills. They are handsomely dressed and deep in thought, the poet holding the painter's walking stick and hat. Overhanging trees and cliffs frame an idealized view of a tumbling stream, mountains, and Kaaterskill Falls in the far distance, cloaking the two men within what art historian Barbara Babcock Lassiter called an "encompassing wilderness." This is the scene lovingly recorded in 1849, soon after Cole's death, by Asher B. Durand, a prominent painter of the Hudson River School, in his *Kindred Spirits*. This much-celebrated work, often cited as one of the principal masterpieces of nineteenth-century American art, evokes the spirit of a culture dedicated to the moral power of wilderness as the embodiment of Eden.

Along the Hudson, God long served as conservation's copilot. Cole, in the words of the environmental historian David Stradling, "was steeped in the romantic idea that in nature one could find God," whose "power could be felt in an overwhelming sensation that drove many nineteenth century tourists to tears." Cole had traveled widely in his search for the most evocative wilderness scenes to paint and discuss, finally putting down deep roots at his farm, called Cedar Grove, in Catskill on the river. He became the doyen of the Hudson River School of painters and encouraged many of them to follow him in sketching and painting the region's poetic landscapes that he discovered and revered. He deplored "savages of the axe" who "destroyed nature's beauty without substituting that of art."

Bryant likewise worshipped God in nature and ascribed value to wilderness, influencing the thought and writings of others—Thoreau, Emerson, James Fenimore Cooper, Washington Irving, Cole himself—who helped define America and especially the Hudson Valley as a persistent Eden. Fictional celebrities such as Cooper's Natty Bumppo and Irving's Rip Van Winkle expressed reverence for the wilderness and did much to spread the word about its heavenly attributes. Both heroes, said author Peter Manning, also "showed the American public that the American wilderness was not only romantic and awesome, but something to be respected and explored."

Such sentiments blossomed during the lush years of the Romantic era, and they endured far longer as a widespread and fervent belief in the importance of preserving scenery and landscapes. As the Storm King battle in the Hudson Highlands brewed, environmental issues eventually trumped "scenery" as principal in the outcome. But one should not discount the great importance of underlying cultural values there and elsewhere in the mix of factors contributing to the Hudson's revival—and of their considerable economic strength. From the days of the great battles over the Palisades to the more recent efforts to avoid disfiguring the outlook from Frederic Church's Olana, the power of views and viewsheds, and the strong urge to protect them, centrally motivated many of the leaders in many of the struggles. Scenery-based accomplishments, including especially those fostering the flowering of cultural tourism, have resulted in many positive gains for the new Hudsonian economy.

Head slightly cocked to one side, hair slicked straight back, mustache tidily trimmed above a playful smile, face smooth, eyes alert, Peter Stern faces the camera to recount a few of his many "thrilling and sad memories" as president of the Storm King Art Center. This magnificent outdoor sculpture garden, celebrating its fiftieth anniversary in 2011, stretches across more than five hundred acres of undulating green landscape nestled between Storm King Mountain to the east and Schunnemunk Mountain to the west. On the carefully tended grounds, as well as in a small headquarters building that replicates a chateau in Normandy, are fine examples of work by famous artists: Isamu Noguchi, Alexander Calder, David Smith, Mark di Suvero, Louise Nevelson, Maya Lin.

Over the years the art center grew from modest origins to become one of the world's foremost sculpture gardens, described thus in a 1987 *Christian Science Monitor* article: "Storm King stands head and shoulders above other American sculpture parks—in size, the beauty of its grounds, the quality and range of its collection, and the care it takes in harmonizing art with its surroundings." Its evolution is an absorbing story, especially since neither of the founders—Stern and his ex-father-in-law, the jovial industrialist and country squire Ralph E. ("Ted") Ogden—began with any formal education in art history or curatorial expertise. But with great energy and ample supplies of good advice, they ploughed their way forward to ever-greater success.

In his lengthy video memoirs, as well as in a 2003 lecture given at the Chautauqua Institution, Stern plumbed the origins of the idea. From the 1930s through the early post–World War II years, Ogden's Star Expansion Bolt Company was highly successful and made him a fortune. In 1956 he moved the company's factory, where various types of metal fasteners were manufactured, from grimy Bayonne, New Jersey, to the small farming community of Mountainville in the Hudson Highlands. Ogden made this his principal residence, becoming a major donor to local institutions, often anonymously, and adding to acquisitions of farmland that his father had started making in the region. An engineer, Ogden was fascinated by large machines, by the mechanics of farming. And, said Stern, he had "a sense of making landscape useful." He liked scale.

By the late 1950s Ogden had fastened onto the idea of founding a new institution that would fill a cultural void in the region by "presenting the dramatic story of the Hudson River in museum form." In 1958 Ogden bought for this purpose the beautiful estate belonging to New York lawyer Vermont Hatch, who had died. "By certain institutional and individual financing the home and a substantial portion of the surrounding landscape were purchased for the art center—and thus the Storm King Art Center came into existence," reported the Cornwall *Local*. Included in the deal were twenty-three acres of land and a handsome chateaulike structure, designed by New York architect Maxwell Kimball, sited on a hilltop with commanding views and built in 1930 of native fieldstone. It featured beautiful wooden parquet floors and other amenities.

Late in the 1950s the balance of power shifted from Ogden to Peter Stern, a Renaissance man with an unusual upbringing and superb taste. After a pre–World War II sojourn in Romania, his German-Jewish family caught the last ship out of the Mediterranean in June 1940 and settled in Scarsdale, New York. Young Peter graduated from Harvard and grappled with the question of how to become secretary of state, winning an MA in international relations from Columbia University before switching to the Yale Law School. As a young lawyer based in Washington, Stern solved a problem for Ted Ogden who, says Stern, "considered me a miracle worker." Later, in rapid succession, Stern married Ogden's daughter Joan, moved to New York, and joined Star Expansion, soon becoming its president.

In 1956 Ogden vowed to Stern that never again would he come to the office to do business. "I'm going to have some fun traveling in Europe and learning about art," he told Stern. Likewise, he handed over the incipient art center, asking Stern to become chairman and president, taking care of administrative matters, so that "I could have fun running the artistic end." So at age twenty-eight Stern was in control of both the company and the art center, remaining in charge for many years after he and Joan divorced. He described to Ogden the advantages of setting up the art center as a tax-exempt nonprofit and the process of achieving a suitable Internal Revenue Service determination. "How do you get one of those?" Ogden asked. Stern told him, and it was soon done. Stern, a gifted man with great intelligence and charm and a wonderful sense of humor, was well on the way toward fulfilling his goal to make the place "truly public."

In July 1960 the art center was formally launched with an exhibition of works by classic Hudson River painters and remained open several afternoons a week with no admission charge. The show stayed up for six weeks and achieved an attendance of 750. In 1967 came an exhibition of works by Winslow Homer, who spent time in the Hudson Valley before he concentrated on Maine, attracting an audience of 5,000 and winning praise from the *New York Times* as an "extraordinary little experiment."

Gradually, the focus narrowed, and the center's ambitions grew. In 1967, after Ogden bagged "in one swoop" a collection of thirteen David Smith pieces, Stern said, "We wouldn't in the least mind being known as one of the places to see Smith's work. As a small museum we're better off collecting the work of an artist in depth than trying to acquire a smattering of everything." Over the years came further tightening decisions: that the artist has to be primarily a sculptor; that most of the pieces on display be primarily those to be placed outdoors, with indoor spaces left to a supporting role; that the works be relatively large in keeping with the grand size of the site, and that from a maintenance standpoint they be capable of surviving outdoors, withstanding rugged winters and steamy summers.

As Ogden and Stern refined their collecting goals, after 1974 with the help of keen-eyed director and curator David Collens, strong-armed from many years of helping workers wrestle heavy structures onto pads sited on the grounds with exacting precision, they also paid increasing attention to treasuring and enhancing the landscape—preserving and creating vistas and views, hiding parked cars by means of clever tree pruning, making a top priority for acquisitions that they interact gracefully with the surroundings. Assisted in major ways by the landscape architect William A. Rutherford Sr., who, Stern says "transformed our landscape," they worked to undo the site's original golf course look and create pathways of short grass between stands of long grasses echoing the hayfields of the farming days. They planted acres of wildflowers and used trees "for beauty, shade, and definition," Stern has noted. To counter what he calls the "brutal" disfiguration of the property when two million cubic yards of gravel were removed to create roadbed for the nearby New York State Thruway, under construction during the 1950s, major surgery turned disaster into opportunity, as Stern put it. Maya Lin's gracefully undulating eleven-acre land sculpture on that part of the grounds, entitled *Storm King Wavefield*, "transformed a gravel pit into a majestic earthwork," says Collens. Lin visited several times in the mid- and late 2000s, walking the grounds before reaching a decision about what to place there. The result, opened in May 2009, twists the mind. From above, my wife and I watched people we thought were children clambering up and down Lin's succession of hills. Emerging, they turned into full-size adults.

Other prominent artists, from Richard Serra to Noguchi to Andy Goldsworthy, with his exuberant "wall that went for a walk" winding through the grounds, has made special efforts to interact gracefully with their works' surroundings. Among those selected for a 2010 exhibition celebrating the art center's fiftieth anniversary, most do work with a distinctly environmental tilt. Especially notable is *Stream: A Folded Drawing,* an intricate piece by Stephen Talasnik. It consists of about three thousand bamboo poles forming a kidney-shaped structure 15 feet high by 115 feet long that appears to be rolling or almost floating down the hillside on which it was assembled. *Mirror Fence,* by the widely known and respected Alyson Shotz, resembles a traditional picket fence, but what you see is reflected grass and reflections of viewers walking by. "It's a fence but not really a fence," she said at a site visit with art center members. "It raises the question of what is solid and what is not, of what is a fence. It drifts in and out of substance."

These choices reflect the management's ever-growing preoccupation with the relationship between the art and its surroundings. As Stern put it in the art center's handsome 2000 book *Earth, Sky, and Sculpture,* "Ted Ogden's and my responses to the beauty of our landscape and the drama of monumental sculpture challenged us over time to harmonize these two assets . . . we added a sculpture only if it interacted well with the landscape and other sculptures." Art center board member Peter Beinstock took the conceit a big step further. "Perhaps the greatest sculpture of all," he wrote, "is the brilliantly crafted landscape itself."

All this has accrued to great benefit for the art center's visitors, who during the 2009 season (April–October) doubled in number (to seventy-five thousand) from the previous year. As many as twenty-three hundred have come in a single day. They can now enjoy far more than the basic pleasure of walking the grounds. There is a Tourmobile. Bikes are available for rental. A cafe has opened near one of the parking areas. There are docent tours, concert lectures, a comprehensive education program. In every sense the art center has not only filled a void but taken on the trappings of a full-fledged museum. More change is bound to come. Ted Ogden has long since died, and in 2009 Peter Stern, having decreed that he too was entitled to "have fun," stepped down after forty-eight years and handed over the presidency to his son John. Daughters Beatrice and Lisa have joined the staff. All have their own ideas, and surprisingly, many of them echo the thoughts and passions of the region's nineteenth-century transcendentalists.

Only half an hour's drive away from the Storm King Art Center, across the Newburgh–Beacon Bridge, is Dia:Beacon. For many years a Nabisco factory, this place has been transformed into a lively contemporary art museum and an emblem for a community that has with notable success been reconnected with its own long-abandoned shorefront. The revived Beacon has evolved and prospered, a story told separately in the chapter that follows, with Dia:Beacon playing a key part in the town's transformation.

Likewise enlivening the mid-Hudson scene is Bard College in Annandale, with a magnetic president, Leon Botstein, at the helm. Musicologist, orchestra conductor, champion fund-raiser, Botstein has been a college president ever since, at the tender age of twenty-three, he took that job at the now-defunct Franconia College in New Hampshire. In 1975, not yet thirty, he became head of Bard, a small, laid-back private college with about seven hundred students that was linked to the Episcopal Church and had long emphasized music and the performing arts. Soon after he arrived, says Botstein, he called on Vincent Astor's first wife Helen Dinsmore Huntington, who at the time was a leading Hudson grande dame.

"The region was mired in the past," she told me. "It can't see beyond its backyard; it's a Cherry Orchard environment. But it does have a future in culture and education." When IBM's major Poughkeepsie plant shut down, leaving Bard as a leading Dutchess County employer, Botstein says, "The city fathers came to us and asked what to do. The answer was cultural tourism. Laurance Rockefeller asked about that too—the only time I ever met him. We needed new space for it. The original idea was an outdoor shed. We studied that but concluded that it wouldn't do. No one anymore wants to sit outdoors and listen to lousy quality sound. This is a ferociously competitive world. So what we needed was a signature building, not only for music but also for our theater, dance, and film programs."

The result was the striking Frank Gehry–designed Richard B. Fisher Center for the Performing Arts on campus, built with public as well as private funds. With the Fisher Center as the principal venue, Bard now puts on an ambitious seven-week summer festival called Summerscape. The program is built around Botstein's professional American Symphony Orchestra, which also regularly performs in New York City. A recent innovation is the Bard College Conservatory of Music, where a student can double-major in music and something else and, as at the Marlboro Music Festival in Vermont, perform alongside faculty members and other well-seasoned professional musicians. Bard also features adventuresome theater and dance programs—not uniformly successful, one hears, often again blending student and professional talent. Recently on campus, for example, was the talented dancer Bill T. Jones and his well-known company.

Under Botstein's gifted and energetic leadership Bard has achieved national and international status with programs and affiliations all over and a one hundred million dollar budget. Closer to home, Botstein continues, "We've always wanted to exploit our location and our good fortune to be in a historically and environmentally important place." Unlike students at many other colleges who rarely stray off the reservation, Bard's mingle freely with the local community. By design five hundred of them live off campus, tasting what Botstein calls "the authenticity of a rural experience." They kayak and bike and go camping. They participate in the community. For the benefit of migrant workers in the region, they produce the only Spanish-language publication around. It works the other way, too: One-third of the attendance at Bard's cultural events is local. The college also runs an athletic club for the community as what Botstein calls a "quality of life contribution."

Down the road in Poughkeepsie is Vassar College, long a stately enclave for seriously scholarly women, now also a bustling coed liberal arts school with lively programs both in the arts and in the environmental field. Vassar boasts a top-quality art museum, the 36,500 square-foot Frances Loeb Lehman Art Center designed by Cesar Pelli and open since 1993. Free of charge to the public, the center has a wide-ranging collection of some eighteen thousand artworks, including important Hudson Valley paintings donated by the college's founder, beer baron Matthew Vassar. Like Bard, Vassar has excellent programs in music, dance, and theater.

Much of what's exciting at Vassar involves the distinguished presidency of Frances Daly Fergusson, which spanned twenty years, from 1986 to 2006. An architectural historian, she worked closely with Pelli to help make Vassar's campus what she calls "one of the most coherent and beautiful in America." She raised more than $750 million, an impressive sum for a small college. She tightened links with Poughkeepsie, a downtrodden community when she arrived.

Each summer the college, in partnership with New York Stage and Film, puts on the adventuresome Powerhouse Theater program, which founder and now big-league film producer Leslie Urdang calls a "starry eyed undertaking hatched in 1984 to provide emerging artists the wherewithal to develop and present new work in readings, workshops, and productions." Powerhouse has attracted such top talent as Meryl Streep (a Vassar grad), Sam Waterston, and others of similar stature. Many stars have camped out in student dorms as part of the experience.

A less well-known but brightening light, on the east bank of the river just north of downtown Poughkeepsie, is Marist College. "The campus and view at any season is gorgeous," wrote one student reviewer with more fervor than grammatical skill. One campus feature is the twelve-acre riverside Longview Park. Home for the college's high-ranked crew team, and bikers and hikers as well, the park is open to the public and well used. The college has enjoyed steady growth in size and prestige since the Marist brothers founded it in 1905. On campus currently, studying in myriad fields, are some forty-one hundred undergraduates, one thousand graduate students, and forty-one hundred adults enrolled in continuing education programs.

Marist consistently ranks well in the college ratings by *U.S. News* and in many other college ratings listings. Its excellent library, built in 2000, is especially rich in Hudsonia. Among its local holdings is an extensive collection of materials having to do with the Con Edison/Storm King dispute. Affiliated with Marist is the Hudson River Valley Institute, publisher of the handsome, informative, and readable *Hudson River Valley Review*.

If these academic institutions do much to stimulate life and economic activity in the region, another big cultural boost comes from its proliferation of historical houses that are open to the public. Running these in the black is not for the fainthearted, as I learned from many years of membership on the board of Historic Sotterley, proprietor of an early-eighteenth-century plantation house and grounds along a beautiful stretch of the Patuxent River in southern Maryland. Sotterley has everything: a stunning site complete with nesting bald eagles that are frequently seen, a splendid garden, a juxtaposed mansion house and slave quarters that dramatically make history come alive. It's an easy drive down from Washington or Baltimore.

But the fragile old buildings on the grounds require constant attention. Education, marketing, and public information require funds that are always in short supply. Violent storms occur with disturbing frequency. A microburst from 2011's Hurricane Irene uprooted thirty trees on the grounds and damaged several buildings, including the principal dwelling on the plantation. Sotterley soldiers on with great energy and determination, but the abyss is seldom far away. So it is as well with the Hudson's myriad assortment of castles, mansions, artists' residences and studios, and architectural curiosities that crowd its banks. "These are the buildings that make our heads ache but our hearts sing," said John Winthrop Aldrich, formerly the state's deeply knowledgeable historic preservation deputy commissioner, at a recent gathering of the faithful.

The Hudson River Valley National Heritage Area program was declared by a 1996 act of Congress in recognition of the region's importance as "the landscape that defines America." It is one of forty-nine such areas throughout the United States that function in partnership with the National Park Service. The Hudson program promotes and helps manage some ninety natural heritage sites, more than half of them house museums, in 250 communities located within the 154-mile tidal estuarial portion of the river, from New York City's northern border to the mouth of the Mohawk River near Albany. The law groups the area's attractions in three categories: Freedom and Dignity highlights sites that figured in the Revolutionary War and in the life of President Franklin D. Roosevelt. Under Nature and Culture are gathered many homes in the valley that were occupied by famous artists and writers of the nineteenth century. Some of these, or their gardens, were designed by the architects Andrew Jackson Downing, Calvert Vaux, or Alexander Jackson Davis. The Corridor of Commerce grouping emphasizes places such as the West Point Foundry that figured prominently in the Hudson's industrial past. Historic Hudson Valley, a Rockefeller dependency, runs six houses, including the grand six-story stone house called Kykuit in the Pocantico Hills that was the family's country home for four generations.

Other prominent National Heritage dwellings were built or rebuilt by notables of the Golden Age with familiar names: robber baron Jay Gould's Gothic revival chateau called Lyndhurst in Tarrytown, FDR's Springwood in Hyde Park, Washington Irving's Sunnyside, Frederick Vanderbilt's fifty-four-room mansion. Seven generations of Livingstons occupied one residence called Clermont in Germantown, and members of the family built houses on dozens of other estates arrayed along the river's east bank, many of them commanding magnificent views of the Catskills to the west. I have a special fondness for the family's beautifully located Montgomery Place in Annandale, again with a splendid river view, where my daughter's wedding took place on a breathlessly beautiful summer afternoon. "They Had It and Flaunted It," headlined the *New York Times*, whose breathless travel writer had completed a flower-bedecked, candlelit Christmas holiday tour of the region's gaudiest palaces.

Wint Aldrich, an indefatigable champion of these great houses, frequents a somewhat bedraggled forty-three-room one called Rokeby. The place was once "populated," the *Times* reported, "by a colorful but mostly impecunious cast of Livingston and Astor descendants—who are struggling, sometimes with each other, to keep the house from falling down while tending to their own deeply individual destinies." For all the yellowing paint flaking off the walls, Aldrich cherishes Rokeby. He places it in a broad context, emphasizing both the employment and the revenues that these properties generate, well over a billion dollars a year directly, and the hotel and restaurant revenues that circulate as by-products. The numbers were up in 2010, despite or perhaps because of the Great Recession, which may have prompted many vacationers to stay closer to home than usual.

Aldrich finds hope in the swarms of enthusiasts who work as docents or costumed volunteers at the houses, helping to keep alive important slivers of American history and culture. He is saddened when feathers get ruffled in this small but energetic world, as happened when Historic Hudson Valley closed down Montgomery Place on the grounds that it could not afford the site's five hundred thousand dollar annual operating cost and at a board meeting discussed selling all or part of the property. Flying rumors infuriated the previous owners, Livingston family descendants who, as in the instance of the Stillmans' dealings with Harvard over Black Rock Forest, thought they had put their cherished property in safe hands when they sold out to the Rockefellers. But generally, though some of the old mansions open to the public have fallen into disrepair, enough people stop by to keep the balls rolling—and Wint Aldrich precariously happy.

Not all the houses are grand historical mansions. A contrasting example is a remarkable site called Manitoga on a hillside near the Bear Mountain Bridge in Putnam County. This is where the designer Russel Wright, who marketed a simple post–World War II lifestyle fashioned around his plastic American Modern dinnerware, built a replica of a quarry. On the pond's flank Wright then placed a breathtaking house called Dragon's Rock that tucks into its space in the manner of Frank Lloyd Wright's (no relation) Fallingwater in Pennsylvania. Russel Wright similarly planned his retreat to be "in and of the landscape, not imposed on it," as Robert Schonfeld wrote in his book *Russel Wright: Creating American Lifestyle*. A large tree rises from the kitchen, flanked by stone steps leading up to the dining area. Manitoga's Russel Wright Design Center bills itself as "the only 20th Century modern home open to the public in New York State." Much goes on in and around the house, including tours, hikes along carefully preened trails winding though the site's seventy-five acres of woodland, and summer camps and activities for children and adults.

One illuminating example of history's role in the Highlands is Foundry Cove, a pretty little wetland just south of Cold Spring. In 1818, after President James Madison had complained that the United States lacked domestic suppliers of cannons for wartime use, a heavy industrial ironworks called the West Point Foundry set up massive operations here. Water from a creek spun a thirty-six-foot diameter wheel driving giant lathes to make iron from local ore and build steam engines, locomotives, and ironclad ships. During the Civil War the site was famous for its production of the mighty Parrott Gun, one model of which could miraculously hurl a three-hundred-pound projectile at a target nine thousand yards away. President Lincoln came to visit this famous plant.

But after the war changing needs and technologies closed down the operation. Where once up to fifteen hundred people had worked, there came a long decline. After operations stopped completely in 1911, the site fell gradually into disarray. It became a dump, with only one standing nineteenth-century brick administrative office building serving as a reminder of the major installation that had been there.

A later owner in the 1950s to 1970s, a company called Marathon Battery, manufactured batteries there using a process involving the deadly drainpipe release into the Hudson of two hundred thousand gallons of cadmium- and nickel-laden water a day. Declared a Superfund site by the EPA, Foundry Cove then underwent a long cleanup. Subsequently, it once again fell dormant, with locals using the cove as a favored dog-walking destination as the factory installations little by little disappeared underground and under fallen tree leaves from a regenerating forest.

In 1996 Scenic Hudson bought eighty-seven acres of the cleaned-up site on the grounds of its being a striking example of nineteenth-century heavy-industry design. With assistance from an industrial archaeologist, Todd Martin from Michigan Technological University, Scenic Hudson is raising $3.5 million from public and private sources to transform it into an outdoor museum, a park, and a recreation area for the community. Care is being taken to have the project, now called the West Point Foundry Preserve, meet community needs, such as smooth traffic flow along Cold Spring's narrow, busy Main Street. Says Scenic Hudson's project manager, Rita Shaheen: "We've worked hard to make sure that there are no negative impacts, especially when it comes to roads."

No summary of the region's historical sites would be complete without featuring the artist Frederic Edwin Church and what Joan Davidson calls "wonderfully eccentric" Olana, the distinctive residence he lovingly created on the river near the town of Hudson. He lived and worked there for many years. The care Church took to fashion what had been a "hardscrabble landscape," says Olana Partnership director Sara Griffen, extends far beyond the lavishly appointed house to form what the partnership calls "three dimensional art"—a truly integrated environment embracing architecture, art, and landscape unmatched by any other nineteenth-century mansion in the region, with an interior containing an assortment of "Oriental" objects and a bank of south-facing windows yielding splendid panoramic views down and across the river.

In a rapidly developing region with a growing population, Olana's viewshed came close to giving way to sprawl during the 1960s when hard-up Church family members planned to sell off the property. But an unlikely savior, Smith College art history professor David Huntington, managed to raise $350,000 toward an asking price of $500,000. Then New

York State governor Nelson Rockefeller was persuaded to chip in the full amount, leaving what Huntington had raised for badly needed maintenance and Olana to a relatively secure future as a state historical park.

More than any other of the region's historical sites, Olana manifests most clearly the importance of protecting not just dwellings and landscapes but also the integrity of entire viewsheds, defined as natural landscapes that can be seen and appreciated from more than a single viewpoint. At a "Framing the Viewshed" symposium held in April 2011 near Olana, the Olana Partnership gathered more than two hundred of the usual suspects to celebrate and reaffirm their vows to save these wondrous places and especially Olana. "This thing called 'landscape' is more precious than gold and as fragile as life itself," said one participant, Olana staff member Linda McLean. Charles Birnbaum, founder and president of the Cultural Landscape Foundation, stressed the importance of seeing Olana's viewshed and "borrowed scenery" as integral to its quest for UNESCO designation as a World Heritage site. Success would be a "powerful tool for how Olana presents itself and manages its own change."

"Olana is all about the views," said Olana Partnership board member Mark Prezorski.

One way or another, each of these cultural institutions, and scores of others, add heft to the region's economy. Counties keep careful track of growing numbers of visitors and what they spend, especially in the "staycation" economic climate of recent years. Wint Aldrich speaks of the doubtless existence of a "very vital intellectual and cultural community" in Dutchess and Columbia Counties. Olana brings some eight million dollars a year into the local economy and supports some fifteen hundred jobs.

An old economic study done at Marist College confirmed that visitors to cultural and natural resources in the valley numbered 1.5 million to 2 million annual tourists, not counting school groups. They came from relatively close by and were mostly day-trippers or weekenders. They were mostly older, relatively well-off people with college degrees. I could not find anywhere a study that embraces the economic consequences of cultural tourism for the Hudson Valley as a whole, including aggregate attendance at museums and academic institutions, as well as at the historical sites. Doubtless the figures would be impressive.

From faraway there comes news of one community that, surprisingly, gets it about cultural development. It is, says the *New York Times*, the Russian town of Perm, nine hundred miles west of Moscow. Better known as the gateway to Siberia and the place where many Soviet-era dissidents were last seen before disappearing into the gulag, said the *Times*, Perm now seeks to establish itself as "a key stop on Russia's cultural map, opening gallery and performance spaces the way it once produced nuclear ballistic missiles ... the broad esplanade running from the city's main square has become the site of almost continuous international art, theater, and music fairs during the summer."

The shift came about when, in 2004, a new provincial governor began looking for ways to keep young people from moving away and decided to budget for culture, setting aside fifty-three million dollars, or 3 percent of his budget, to build infrastructure and "branding" mechanisms for this purpose. Who knows whether the provincial master plan will work, concluded the paper's reporter, Finn-Olaf Jones, but "there is something undeniably fun and dramatic in traveling to the edge of Siberia to find that a city once so forbidding has suddenly become a vibrant sanctuary for artists."

Poughkeepsie, with an abundance of nearby cultural wealth and the Walkway Over the Hudson as a new springboard to build on, could do worse than give the model a try.

CHAPTER 7

Rescuing the Shoreline

BACK IN THE 1990S THE TOWN OF BEACON ON THE HUDSON'S EAST bank displayed all the symptoms of postindustrial distress. Set on a hillside with arresting views of Storm King Mountain to the southwest and the busy Newburgh-to-Beacon bridge to the north, the town had lost its factories and its soul. Crime and poverty were endemic. Business had dwindled along what had long ago been a thriving Main Street before shopping malls opened a few minutes' drive to the north. Only fifteen years before, Main Street merchant John Gilvey told travel writer Kristen Hinman in 2010, the street had been "all flophouses, brothels and crack dens." At one old market, you could buy crack over the counter.

"Nobody in their right mind came to town, day or night," Hinman added in her *Washington Post* article. Along the shoreline, cut off from the rest of town by busy rail tracks and auto traffic, one choice site had become a junkyard and an oil storage facility. Another served as a landfill. Abandoned industrial buildings were rusting away all along the waterfront, except at the small Riverfront Park built on a landfill at the northern end of the town's shoreline.

But in just the past few years, thanks to the concurrent and well-coordinated efforts of several strong forces, this derelict coast has been dramatically revived. Main Street has blossomed with restaurants, cafes, and stores, including Gilvey's beach glass and glassblowing studio. The giant Dia:Beacon Art Center, with 240,000 square feet of exhibition space, has, since it opened in 2003, attracted streams of visitors to its site near the shore. Many come by train, arriving at a renovated terminal and taking an easy walk uphill to Dia and Main Street or across toward waterside attractions.

Several parks and hiking trails now occupy what had been wasted riverfront acreage. The new Scenic Hudson–sponsored Long Dock Park, a $16.5 million project, spreads across twenty-five acres of Beacon shorefront. The nonprofit Beacon Institute for Rivers and Estuaries, a scientific research organization, has set up its headquarters on Main Street and its new Center for Environmental Innovation and Education at Denning's Point, formerly a much-visited beach-going and swimming peninsula before pollution killed it and foreign competition stamped out the industries installed there. Ferries once again link downtown Beacon with downtown Newburgh on the Hudson's west bank. Sailboats bob at their moorings, and kayakers paddle about. These scenes confirm that once-shoddy Beacon has become a notable example of how quickly gains can be scored when a Hudson Valley community reconnects with its abandoned shoreline.

Normally, you might think, such a spirited revival would come about as a consequence of energetic citizens moved to goad politicians and sluggish bureaucrats into action. Not so in the case of Beacon, where it was public-sector leadership at the state and local levels that opened the way. To begin with, there was the long-standing aspiration on the part of New York State's awkwardly named Office of Parks, Recreation, and Historic Preservation (OPRHP) to get hold of Denning's Point. This sixty-four-acre parcel had been well-kept farmland back in the early 1900s and later a busy industrial site. By the late 1980s, wrote Jim Heron in his detailed book *Denning's Point: A Hudson River History,* the peninsula had long since fallen into the hands of the Noesting Pin

Ticket Company, manufacturer of paper clips and various other fasteners and devices.

When the company faltered thanks to foreign competition and resolved to abandon the site, some of Beacon's old-guard politicos wanted to keep the property on the tax rolls and find another company or developer to take over. But there had been a long history of discussions between OPRHP and Noesting's conservation-minded CEO, William Griffiths Sr. In 1988 a firm offer from a developer to buy the property for six million dollars brought the matter to a head. Griffiths gave the state a chance to match the developer's offer. Soon the deed was done, with the state trumping local opposition and Denning's being added to the Hudson Highlands State Park. "Everybody had won," reported Heron. "The State of New York owns valuable parkland, and the Griffiths [family] received a fair price for Denning's Point and delivered it into the hands of people dedicated to preserving it from inappropriate development."

Creative thinking within the Albany bureaucracy had helped support citizen aspirations to trump St. Lawrence Cement and restore the downtrodden town of Hudson. Back in the 1980s the same state officials came to Beacon's rescue. State coastal resources planner Steve Resler and his colleagues, especially state secretary of state Alexander Treadwell, had the ear of then governor George Pataki, a staunch environmentalist of long standing. They became fastened on the idea of strengthening coastal communities by reconnecting abandoned shorefronts with the towns that had turned their backs on them.

Under a state law they fashioned, the Waterfront Revitalization of Coastal Areas and Inland Waterways Act, local communities were given the opportunity to craft Local Waterfront Revitalization Programs (LWRPs) conforming to no fewer than forty-four state policies governing land use, pollution control, natural resources, use of recreational and scenic assets, and so on. Once a local LWRP had been approved, the state required that all shorefront actions by all state and federal agencies be "consistent" (the key word) with the local program's policies and purposes. The "clear intent" of the legislation "was to do what the policy says," says Resler, now officially retired but still busy consulting on coastal management issues. "If anything conflicts, you can't do it." Resler called the process "reverse federalism." Federal policy support for Beacon's process of bottom-up, environmentally sensitive shoreline planning could be found within several laws, including the Clean Water Act and especially the groundbreaking 1972 Coastal Zone Management Act.

In Beacon, with then mayor Clara Lou Gould as what Resler calls "a fantastic driving force," public servants and cadres of citizen volunteers, with careful guidance from Resler and other state officials, sat down in the late 1980s to compose the community's LWRP. It was approved at all necessary levels in 1991–92. The phone book–size document deplores the sad state of Beacon's "deteriorated and underused" waterfront, lack of harbor dredging, an old ferry pier that had become "both dangerous and an eyesore," the ubiquitous presence of "scrub vegetation and dumped materials," lack of adequate water and sewer systems, and so on. Scores of remedial activities, all adhering to the consistency standard, are advocated. Most significantly, the LWRP overrides a 1974 Development Plan that had earmarked most of Beacon's shorefront for "heavy industrial" use. Instead, all "heavy industrial" zoning would be eliminated, and new zoning categories would encourage "waterfront park" and "waterfront development" districts with carefully reasoned allocations favoring recreation, light industry, the restoration of trans-Hudson ferry service that had been terminated in 1963, and making parkland out of long-abandoned spaces in choice locations.

One private citizen with a particular interest in New York State's 1988 acquisition of Denning's Point was the energetic John Cronin. A fast-moving, all-purpose environmentalist with a keen sense of how to get widespread attention, Cronin has an unusual past. For a while as a restless teenager, he tried college but dropped out, then wanted to be a ballet dancer. Later, as Alex Wilkinson chronicled in a 1987 *New Yorker* profile, he went on the road, washed dishes, slept in the car. Returning East after a western swing, he hooked up with the Hudson River Fishermen's Association. In 1983 that relationship led to his becoming the Hudson Riverkeeper—first of what is now a chain of more than two hundred waterkeepers the world over, with high-visibility leadership from Robert F. Kennedy Jr. It was Cronin who spotted Exxon vessels illegally flushing oily water tanks in mid-Hudson, took the company to court, and eventually landed a big cash settlement to invest in protecting the Hudson.

Having given up his Riverkeeper position after seventeen years of diligent Hudson monitoring, Cronin turned his attention to fashioning a giant nonprofit scientific research and policy analysis shop that would use innovative high-technology methods to study the Hudson and aquatic systems everywhere. The idea won enthusiastic attention from Pataki, who in his 2000 State of the State speech included a provision for what environmental blogger Andrew Revkin characterized as a "world-class science center along the Hudson—a kind of Woods Hole Oceanographic Institution for rivers." Pataki, whose government pumped twenty-five million dollars into the project toward anticipated total funding of twice that, appointed Cronin as executive director of what later became the Beacon Institute for Rivers and Estuaries.

The Institute then cut a deal with OPRHP to occupy and renovate a crumbling four-thousand-square-foot building on Denning's Point and brought in the distinguished Gensler architectural firm to do the job. The resulting Center for Environmental Innovation and Education, festooned with high-tech gadgetry and green design features, opened with great fanfare in 2008. But after Pataki left office, and as the Great Recession caused reductions in private philanthropies' budgets, the Institute faltered. As of early 2012, it was largely defunct and Cronin was gone. For the local community, though, legal access to the river and Denning's Point, via improved walking trails and pathways, had been achieved for the first time since 1685.

Said the *Christian Science Monitor:* "The 325-mile waterway is slated to undergo the most intense scientific scrutiny of any major river in the United States." For the local community legal public access to the river and the Denning's Point shoreline, via improved walking trails and pathways, has also been achieved for the first time since 1685.

An unlikely hero in the effort to bring back Beacon's shoreline is Michael Govan, director of the Dia Art Foundation from 1994 to 2006 and currently director of the Los Angeles County Museum of Art. His problem was a simple one: Dia, founded in 1974, had amassed a formidable collection consisting mostly of works by prominent artists, many large in size, from the 1960s on. Despite artful juggling of exhibition and storage spaces in Manhattan's Chelsea district and elsewhere, Dia had come to need what then *New York Times* reporter (columnist as of 2011) Joe Nocera called a "gargantuan" structure to store and display its permanent collection.

So at age thirty-one and as a pilot, Govan took to the air in search of new space. His good friend the fluorescent light artist Dan Flavin, formerly a resident of Garrison, had told Govan of the wonders of the Hudson Highlands. One day they flew upriver, passing over the Bear Mountain Bridge and such fanciful old buildings as Dick's Castle in Garrison and Bannerman's Castle, a long-abandoned munitions dump on Pollopel Island in the river, facing Storm King Mountain, that is now state parkland.

Approaching the Newburgh–Beacon Bridge, Govan reports, "we looked down at Beacon, and there was this beautiful factory. Dia had a tradition of using old buildings; it had become part of our ethos. It's in my blood. I'd looked around New Jersey and Queens for a place to show our collection, but nothing was quite right, so I had reached a little farther out. Later we found out that International Paper owned the building and that it was for sale. I went up on a rainy spring day and even then could see how beautifully the light came through the north-facing skylights. The site was really depressed. It had become an environmental liability. Nobody had any ideas about what to do with it. So we negotiated directly with International Paper and they ended up giving us the building. Then Governor Pataki came in and got the state to pay 60 or 80 percent of the cleanup costs. It was all a bit by accident." But with about twenty million dollars from bookstore billionaire Leonard Riggio, founder of the Barnes & Noble chain, it all came together, and in 2003 the abandoned 1929 Nabisco box factory opened as Dia:Beacon. Soon, reported art critic Michael Kimmelman, the museum became a "must-see spot on the contemporary art circuit," with attendance exceeding expectations.

Susan Sayre Batton, who in 2010 succeeded Govan as Dia:Beacon's director, underscores her resolve for Dia to remain a good community citizen, with local businesses benefitting to the greatest possible degree from foot traffic between Main Street, the museum, the train station, and the shorefront. Emphasizing her own commitment to outreach and communications in previous museum-world assignments, she says she has spent a fair amount of time strolling Main Street and making cold calls on shop owners. She reports positive reactions even from those located at the eastern end of the street, as far away as it will take you from the museum and the river.

"There's a close relationship," she says. "Main Street closes when Dia closes." Special programs for local schoolchildren get special attention, and the policy of free-admission days has been extended, with some local people being allowed in every single weekend at no charge. The local press does a good job of covering Dia events. Dia directly employs eighty people, most living close by, and also benefits a wide assortment of consultants and service providers. One real estate agent told Batton that she divides the local market into two segments: B.D. (Before Dia) and A.D. Dia's tenth anniversary celebration in 2013 will feature historical coverage of the Dia building when it was a Nabisco box factory.

Batton took me on a quick tour of the premises ("I love it when I can get out of my office and enjoy what's here"). First stop was at a gallery where interns and curators were unfolding and using pieces of fabric designed by the German artist Franz Erhard Walther to examine the "process" of art rather than its "product." Crawling inside to disappear within the folds was obviously fun, with a queue of people awaiting their turn. Then we continued, past rooms full of large sculptures and Andy Warhol paintings, to a south-facing window. On a two-acre meadow outside, South Korean artist Koo Jeong A had placed no fewer than five thousand rhinestones, each sparkling in the late-afternoon sunlight "to create an ephemeral and impermanent shimmering blanket where lights appear, morph and disappear." As we turned away from the window, I made a connection with a suddenly brightly reflecting individual stone, brightly twinkling a vivid orange. Via the little entity within the array, I felt somehow linked to the cosmos. It was heady new enrichment, I felt, for a town that until lately entertained few heavenly aspirations.

An eager participant in the discussions between Dia, International Paper, and Beacon was Ned Sullivan, the talented, high-voltage land preservationist who since 1999 had been leading Scenic Hudson. Equipped with twin degrees from Yale's School of Forestry and Environmental Studies and its School of Organization and Management, Sullivan had served as Maine's environmental commissioner before returning to his native Hudson Valley. Sullivan is a firm believer in the idea that development should occur principally in cities. He thinks that their health can be greatly improved by means of enlightened programs such as what had been undertaken to strengthen Beacon's urban core.

One of Scenic Hudson's major activities now is acquisition of land and its development for parks in and near cities and towns. Not only is Sullivan given credit for "bringing the key players together" in Beacon while the Dia:Beacon project was being negotiated; he has also been a principal force behind the move to transform the town's Long Dock into a world-class park. With the old Riverfront Park on one flank and Denning's Point on the other, and both Dia and the train station close at hand, Long Dock had for quite a while been prospectively a prized crown jewel at the midpoint of the waterfront. But many years of abandonment had resulted in the usual forms of decay.

Back in the 1990s, lured by the promise of Beacon's Local Waterfront Revitalization Plan, Scenic Hudson dipped into its reserve of funds that had been donated by *Reader's Digest* dowager Lila Acheson Wallace for Hudson land preservation to buy and begin to restore twenty-five Long Dock acres. In 2003 it began working with the town, a developer, and public officials to fashion what eventually became the ambitious eighty-five-million-dollar Long Dock Park project. It would include a 166-room waterfront hotel incorporating many green features, a conference center, a public civic plaza, beautiful natural areas, and many shoreline amenities for hikers, boaters, and fishermen. Particularly promising was the up-to-date hotel and conference facility that, says Barnabas McHenry, remains an aching need for the Hudson Highlands.

With much assistance from Beacon mayor Gould and many others, what Scenic Hudson's Long Dock Project Director Margery Groten calls a "creative" financing mechanism was negotiated. Sullivan talked of economic trade-offs: This "very green resource" would bring people to Dia and Main Street and vice versa. Most of all, said Groten, what emerged from an intensive public planning process in which two hundred people participated was the idea that Long Dock should be a public place, not a residential or industrial redevelopment.

In mid-2010, as the closing date for the loan to build the hotel drew closer, the funding package was abruptly put "on hold." But with $8.5 million in Scenic Hudson funds, construction of the surrounding park did begin, with completion achieved in mid-2011. Late in 2010 I donned a hard hat and toured the site with Margery Groten, who expressed little surprise at finding herself working on such a project for a conservation organization.

Though an unexpected mini-tsunami had drenched the site the day before, abetted by the usual 3.5-foot tide, pumps were hard at work, and massive yellow machines were continuing the process of shaping the coming landscape. One barn was being restored for use by environmental education programs. The rest of the site would be left as parkland, connecting by trail with Denning's Point to the south and by road with the railway, Dia, and Main Street. The project was only slightly behind schedule. The demise of the financing for the hotel, and for the extensive landscaping that its developers were prepared to carry out on its portion of the site, came as an admittedly severe blow to the Long Dock team. But with general acknowledgment of a crying need for business-class hotel bedrooms in the Hudson Highlands area—Beacon in 2010 had two bed-and-breakfasts, period—and a splendidly attractive and creative solution all set to go, hopes were high that the hotel financing would fall back into place.

Even with lower Beacon torn up for park construction, a blogger reported that the town, "a dump back in the later 1970s and early 1980s," had become a "really nice place." Clara Lou Gould, mayor from 1989 through 2008, heaps praise on the multiple private-public interactions that occurred along the way. Ned Sullivan and Scenic Hudson were "very helpful," she recalls. So were John Cronin, Michael Govan, Pataki's office in Albany, and various other state officials. Sure, there was opposition from some who wanted the long-vacant old Dia building to start generating real estate tax revenues, and some who preferred hardware stores over art galleries on Main Street. But Gould shrugs off all such complaints: "If you buy art, you need nails. What you lose in real estate taxes you more than make up in higher sales tax revenues. I volunteer at the welcome center, and every day I see how pleased people are, and it's not just tourists but local people, too. The local economy is up. Crime is down. The old ghetto is shrinking. It's gotten to be such a friendly place."

With its big stake in the hotel/conference center project planned for Beacon's Long Dock, Scenic Hudson faces criticism for wandering beyond its mission to save open space and entering an unfamiliar world that is fraught with complications and dominated by the profit motive. Others argue that Sullivan is only practicing what he preaches and that the Beacon hotel, if it is ever built, will doubtless be far greener and healthier than if he were not involved. Adds Margery Groten: "We advocate that communities have a voice in their own planning, and Beacon came to us asking for help. We would only consider the kind of development that is consistent with our mission to make sustainable development an economically feasible reality. I'm not sure we would ever do it again—it's so labor intensive. But we're glad to be here."

Reflecting on all this over a dutifully organic meal at the bustling Home Spun cafe on Beacon's Main Street, I checked my notes for examples of other Hudson towns where waterfront revitalization is happening. The welcome answer: in many places. Some are small, as in the vest-pocket Scenic Hudson Park nestled between the water and the railroad tracks in Irvington, on the river's east bank, close to an Eileen Fisher fashion studio and the Indian Bistro in a restored old brick building by the waterfront. Even the port of Newburgh on the west shore, a poorly run town notorious for having the highest murder rate in New York State, has taken steps to reconnect its once-bustling riverfront to a long-shoddy downtown. In 2005 the weekday Newburgh-to-Beacon ferry service was relaunched. At last count it was attracting four hundred riders a day, at a cost per ride of $1.25. Users were hoping that Saturday and Sunday runs would be added.

Over quesadillas at a cafe in Kingston's busy Rondout Waterfront District, a spacious harbor already boasting five marinas, I discussed development in progress there with Steve Resler. He credits community environmentalists with multiple accomplishments. They have helped plan the restoration of yet another industrial-era boneyard at the mouth of the creek. They forged a successful partnership with a conventional developer, AVR Realty, to fashion its big project, Hudson Landing, more in the style of today's new urbanist pedestrian-friendly aspirations than in the wasteful, ugly patterns and designs of the sprawl era.

In an effort to encourage local communities and developers to take such ideas on board, Scenic Hudson has fashioned a readable and handsome guidebook, *Revitalizing Hudson Riverfronts,* that is available for downloading from the organization's website. Its foreword sets the tone, encouraging users to "direct new growth to municipal centers near transit stations with existing infrastructure so that our open spaces can be preserved for working farms, water and wildlife habitat protection, and recreation." The book also features suggestions as to how shoreline communities along the tidal Hudson can best plan for an expected rise in water level of two to three feet by the end of the current century and perhaps that much again during the 2100s.

So powerful a magnet is local waterfront revival that the concept has risen to the top of the leader board among planners and others forming a "vision" of a healthy future Hudson Valley. In 2009 groups up and down the river celebrated the Hudson Fulton Champlain Quadricentennial. In several respects the shoreline took over center stage in the proceedings. One featured "Quad" project was the Walkway opening. Another was River Day, a giant gathering of fifteen hundred boats of all sorts, led by a replica of Hudson's *Half Moon*, that focused the valley's attention on a splendid asset of which many had been only slightly, if at all, aware. Visiting Newburgh, Quad executive director Tara Sullivan was surprised to discover that many kids did not even know their city was by a river. But, she says, River Day "refreshed everybody's memories and interest and increased their understanding. And now the river is swarming with boats—a few years ago you hardly saw any." For better or worse there are squadrons of snarling Jet Skis out there on a warm summer afternoon.

Following the official termination of the Quad events at the end of 2009, the state announced a "legacy project" to serve as a reminder of the celebration: support for local efforts to build or refurbish "eco-docks" on their shores. Floating docks that rise and fall with the tide, these structures will do much to improve recreational access to the water, to give nonmotorized boaters better access to shoreline communities, and to facilitate recreational paddling. Among the seven hundred thousand dollars in funds awarded to twelve sites were grants to create or improve kayak installations in Hudson, Athens, Troy, Nyack, and Irvington. In Beacon and elsewhere, Scenic Hudson has helped out by building infrastructure for the paddlers, including rental storage spaces for their boats.

One summer afternoon I walked out toward Beacon Point, a site connecting with Long Dock Park that Scenic Hudson had already cleaned up and renovated. At the seaward end of a steel and wood boardwalk are what Scenic Hudson calls "a series of gradual cascading steps which recall the forms of undulating waves." At water's edge is a stairway leading down to the river past a group of concrete cylinders. All this is the work of the Canadian-born, New York–based sculptor George Trakas, an environmentally sensitive sculptor known for designs that highlight natural resource values. Since 1999 Trakas had been working with Scenic Hudson and the Dia Art Foundation, Dia:Beacon's Manhattan-based parent, to design and build a structure, inaugurated in 2007, that would symbolize the closening ties between the city and the river. "Besides underscoring Beacon's working-waterfront past," said local writer David Sokol in *The Architect's Newspaper*, "the artwork also will help inaugurate its postindustrial future."

Approaching the water, I saw some teenage guys relaxing on several of the concrete pillars, fishing and horsing around. Sitting on the stairs leading to the water were two young women in bikinis, each tending a baby happily splashing knee-deep in the river and squealing with delight. As I observed this quiet scene, three people aboard kayaks paddled by, forming a perfect backdrop to a tableau displaying shoreline revitalization at its placid best.

CHAPTER 8

The Locavore Revolution

DURING THE POST–WORLD WAR II YEARS AND UNTIL QUITE RECENTLY, farming in the Hudson Valley seemed likely to disappear all but fully, the victim of a powerful array of contrary forces. The rise of large-scale industrial agriculture put a severe financial squeeze on the smaller family-level operations that were more typical of the region. Development pushed ever more deeply into the countryside as farmers not able to eke out a living sold their lands to make way for shopping centers, residential subdivisions, and sprawl. Local governments, mindless of the sturdy values and economic and environmental benefits of supporting viable farms in their jurisdictions, enacted zoning and fiscal policies that killed many of them.

But in recent years a surprising turnaround has taken place, with the region's small-scale farmers becoming more and more able to hold their own. Public and private support for farmland protection, though flawed, has been on the upswing. There has been an explosion of citizen organizations and coalitions rising up to fight unsustainable development in local Hudson Valley communities and preserve family farms. Most powerful of all, there has emerged the rapid spread of public interest among city dwellers, as well as those in the countryside, in local, organic foods. Bob Lewis, cofounder of the pioneer, fast-growing Greenmarket organization in New York City, proclaims a "revolution" in progress, thanks to the profound changes the locavores have prompted in the relationship between people and food.

Once the Hudson Valley was almost all forested, except for places so rocky or steep that not even trees could grow or small clearings where Indians planted subsistence crops. During colonial times settlers logged furiously to make masts for ships and fashion lumber for buildings and hulls. Farmers followed, planting clearings with fruits and vegetables or fodder for animals. A century ago three-quarters of New York State, and a similar percentage for the Hudson region, remained in farmland. But gathering strength in the 1960s, there followed what an American Farmland Trust report, *Agricultural Economic Development for the Hudson Valley,* published in 2004, called a "steady decline" in the region's farmland, as in many other "urban edge farming regions." Every three days, according to one study, a farm somewhere in New York is still being lost. The American Farmland Trust's researchers had interviewed some who "worry that we will see the complete demise of agriculture in our lifetime" in the Hudson Valley, thanks to a combination of factors that included low prices for farm products, unpredictable weather, and "relentless development pressure."

Despite the grim forecasts, the Hudson's farmers soldier on. In 2010 Judith LaBelle, president of the Glynwood Center, a private nonprofit organization that works to help farmers keep farming, cited and interpreted figures from the US Department of Agriculture's most recent Census of Agriculture:

In 2007 there were 848,214 acres of farmland in the Hudson Valley. That is equivalent to more than 1,300 square miles of land. This is an extraordinary resource, especially in light of its proximity to New York City. Seventeen percent of the region is farmland—again an impressive figure given that the percentage for the state was 24.

The Census also identified more than 5,000 farms in the valley, the vast majority of them owned by individuals or families. They are small and medium sized farms: the average size was 144 acres and more than half were smaller than 70 acres.

Industrial agriculture has long been elbowing aside these typically small farms. Despite generally good soils and a long growing season, Hudson farmers face severe challenges from larger-scale agri-food producers with lower unit costs. At a 2008 food and politics conference, Maya Wiley, director of the Center for Social Inclusion, commented on the irony that while New York State "produces ten times the number of apples eaten in it, 75 percent of apples consumed by New Yorkers are imported from the West Coast or overseas." Dairy and beef operations have severely suffered from larger-scale competition.

Sprawl flourished in the region as farmers with marginal incomes—averaging a meager $13,624 in 2007—sold out to developers and settled for the balmy pleasures of shuffleboard in Florida. One farmer told researchers that the typical transition was a movement "from dairy to hay, to horses or houses." Between 1982 and 1997, according to a Brookings Institution study, upstate New York land was being developed at twelve times the rate of population growth, a trend abetted by massive subsidies for highway construction and widening. What it all meant, according to the Census of Agriculture, was a loss for the valley of a further 10 percent of its farmland between 2002 and 2007. Says LaBelle: "The irony that residential developments are often named for the farms they have replaced becomes ever more poignant."

Local zoning and tax policies often discriminate against these farmers. Zoning decisions are often based on the assumption that farming is a "transitional" land use and that today's farmland will eventually be developed for its "highest and best use" as commercial or residential property. Says LaBelle: "One assessor in our region recently placed a higher assessed value on the portion of a cornfield with a higher elevation, despite the farmer's protest that the corn didn't care about the better view." Such skewed thinking leads to discrimination against farmers whose land belongs in its own zoning and taxing category, rather than bundled in with land bringing a far more lucrative financial return.

For all the forces arrayed against the Hudson's farmers, they remain resourceful and determined. Backing up this grit is a new wave of general appreciation for the economic and environmental benefits of their presence and persistence. In some parts of the country, thanks to overconcentration and lax regulation, farms provoke serious environmental problems. Excessive nutrient runoff from industrial-scale chicken and hog farms into the Chesapeake Bay watershed and North Carolina's bays and estuaries has resulted in serious outbreaks of algal blooms and lethal summer oxygen-deprived "dead zones" where little marine life can survive.

Not so in the Hudson Valley, whose generally well-managed small and tidy fruit, vegetable, and dairy farms for the most part constitute an important component of the region's total supply of open space and freely provide a long roster of "environmental services" for the region. Farms reduce the dangers of erosion and groundwater contamination. When lands are converted from open space to other uses, said the office of state comptroller Thomas P. DiNapoli, communities lose invaluable environmental benefits, including "control of storm water runoff, preservation of surface water quality and stream flows, and infiltration of surface water to replenish aquifers." While precipitation from storms trickles gently into the natural or carefully farmed landscape, 55 percent of it landing on impervious surfaces such as parking lots or roofs becomes fast-moving runoff that causes pollution and erosion and, at a cost to communities, must be managed.

With jurisdictions already suffering from the loss of these tangible environmental benefits, human occupation of previously open spaces brings about additional headaches. New residents flocking into residential subdivisions on former farmland compel rural communities to provide far more in costly services—trash pickup, schools, water, and sewer—than they receive in additional tax revenues. Wider roads lead to more cars, traffic congestion, and higher levels of air pollution contributing to climate change. In a 2010 *Washington Post* op-ed piece, city planners Andres Duany and Jeff Speck added widespread obesity and fatal car crashes to an already lengthy litany of negatives. "You can't grow a green economy on blacktop," the authors concluded.

Nonindustrial farming's importance to the region's local economies, often overlooked, is impressive. Collectively, according to the 2004 American Farmland Trust report, Hudson Valley farms were generating over $230 million in direct sales and had an additional direct economic impact of $300 million. State comptroller DiNapoli notes the continuing importance of farming in the Hudson Valley extending well beyond the farms themselves. In 2007 sales of agricultural commodities in the Hudson Valley, said the comptroller, showed particular strength in a diverse assortment of specialties, including "greenhouse, nursery, floriculture, and sod products" and assorted fruit and vegetable crops such as melons, potatoes, sweet potatoes, cabbages, pumpkins, pears, and the renowned onions grown on Orange County's "black dirt" farms.

In just one small Hudson Valley town, Chatham in Columbia County, resident volunteers conducted a survey and were surprised to discover that local farmers were spending $1.25 million a year on feed, equipment purchase and repair, animal care, and other goods and services. "Without a critical mass of farms in an area," said DiNapoli's 2010 report on economic benefits of open space preservation, "the support businesses that service farms cannot survive, further threatening the viability of farms."

The region's farms provide psychic as well as tangible rewards. Says Chip Allemann, Glynwood's energetic board chair, "Industrial farming has consistently sucked all the life out of many rural communities. When you pull farming out of a rural community, there is no community. Just open space leads to disintegration." In discussions with him and with Glynwood president Judith LaBelle, I got a sense of the many creative ways in which the organization works to keep farmers down on the farm and strengthen rural communities. Headquarters is a 250-acre working farm in Cold Spring that was once the summer residence of the celebrated Perkins family, paragons of careful land stewardship in the valley. From this base, donated by Anne Perkins Cabot to the Open Space Institute, Glynwood's staff of some twenty people strives to fulfill its goals "to empower communities to support farming and conserve farmland, while also working our own land to demonstrate the economic vigor of environmentally sustainable agriculture."

Key to Glynwood's operations is clearly the involvement of LaBelle, an environmental lawyer, teacher, and political scientist with a deep background in Hudson issues. She has worked at Glynwood since 1994 on policy and practice, and her life is a blur of travel between New York City, Cold Spring, and places farther afield. From time to time she visits Normandy, in France, with some of whose farmers Glynwood has formed a partnership, to learn lessons that she can bring home.

On its own farm Glynwood experiments with what Allemann calls "model methods of sustainable farming that others in the region can visit and copy." Classes and retreats are held. Goats, not chemicals, control the spread of invasive plants in hilly places that mechanical mowers cannot reach. Experiments are under way with heritage animal species such as Bourbon Red turkeys, beekeeping to keep an orchard productive, wool processing, ways to use green structures such as straw bales for barn construction, solar power, means of minimizing inputs, and so on. "Diversity protects farms," noted Allemann as he recited the variety of projects. "We're a practice-based think tank."

Beyond the farm's borders, Glynwood seeks to provide infrastructure that is important to individual farmers but beyond their own means. One experiment was a creamery to help satisfy growing consumer interest in locally produced sheep's milk products such as cheese and yogurt. Another: a mobile slaughterhouse that is the first in the Northeast to be licensed by the USDA and is replicable anywhere. The difficulty for the region's producers of organically raised livestock has long been the lack of slaughter capacity within the region and tight schedules at large, faraway facilities. Because their animals are raised outside, LaBelle explained to the *New York Times*, "they don't have as much control over their growth as other people do on feedlots. So even if the animal's not at its optimal weight or condition, they have to keep their appointment." And also lose the right to claim organic certification for the meat.

Already, even though Glynwood's slaughter facility only recently started serving customers, it is demonstrably carrying out its purpose of helping to keep livestock growers in business using organic methods. "I sold my cows off three years ago," grower Jim Eklund told the *Times* after inspecting the Glynwood unit. "Couldn't get 'em processed in a timely manner. It cost me too much to keep up. Saw you doing this. Think this is great. I'm gonna go home and buy cows again."

"Had you told me five years ago that developing a network of high quality slaughterhouses was essential to protecting the Hudson River Valley from sprawl, I would have thought you were nuts," wrote LaBelle. "Now I would think you insightful."

Glynwood is a great believer in the importance of encouraging community people to work together, and Chatham is a good example of the results. Back in 2003, citizens there undertook an assessment as recommended by Glynwood's "Keep Farming" program. Surprising findings included the fact that little local farmland was protected and that much of the land being farmed was not owned by the farmers. Farmers were recruited to serve as members of a Community Agriculture Partnership. Now this body is a town committee empowered to rule on all initiatives that would affect farming. Various efforts were made to inform residents "about local farms, farmers, land preservation techniques and why buying local is so important." An annual Film Fest was launched and an "essential guide" to Chatham farming prepared and distributed.

All these efforts led to the town's elaboration of a Comprehensive Plan responding to development pressures and seeking to improve conditions for local farmers. When completed, the plan included a provision for a 2 percent real estate transfer tax to support a farmland preservation fund. Also recently completed was an Agricultural Preservation Plan that, says LaBelle, "includes the Town's vision and goals for preserving farmland and promoting a viable agriculture economy." Five years after completing the assessment that Glynwood had recommended, Chatham could report zero net loss of farmland.

Another powerful force in arresting farm losses is fast-growing consumer interest in healthy, locally and organically grown food. Farmstands throughout the region are booming, but success is not guaranteed: Of fifteen thousand households in the town of Saugerties, only three hundred patronize the local farmers' market. But a trend is clearly in progress. Direct sales within the valley rose by 36 percent between 2002 and 2007 and have continued to climb since then. Virtually every single person interviewed in one assessment, in Chatham, was a farmstand user. "Don't send me one single new customer," pleaded a farmstand operator in the town of Red Hook. "I'm swamped."

In 2011 *Edible Hudson Valley*, a prosperous looking quarterly magazine "Celebrating Local Foods of the Hudson Valley & Catskills," listed no fewer than eighty-four farmers' markets within the region, from Delaware County to Yonkers on New York City's doorstep. The magazine is chock-full of advertising for a wide variety of goods and services ranging from Hudson Valley single-malt whiskey to local wool and edible landscaping. Another handsome magazine, the *Valley Table*, highlights not only the farms that feature local foods but also the scores of restaurants in the valley that proudly serve them. Enjoying rapid growth are community-supported agriculture programs (CSAs) in which co-op members pay annual fees (or donate work) to receive regular allotments of locally produced food.

Vassar shows how colleges, many of whose students have become passionate about the subject, can offer them on-the-ground opportunities to get involved. Vassar leases 10 acres of land on its 527.5-acre Vassar Farm to the energetic Poughkeepsie Farm Project (PFP), a nonprofit CSA initiative that since 1999 has been supplying healthy local food to four hundred shareholding families as well as to the needy in the community. Vassar students work at the farm either for academic credit or as paid interns. "They can walk here and join the real world without having to go far," says PFP manager Susan Grove. "Of course we have our differences, but basically it's been a good relationship." Academic departments use the farm headquarters, the Priscilla Bullitt Collins Field Station, designed by Cesar Pelli and built in 1995. An environmental education course brings together Vassar students and elementary schoolchildren from the neighborhood. A stream meandering across the handsome, 1,000-acre campus gets close attention from ecology students.

A major force favoring Hudson Valley food producers is New York City's Greenmarket farmers' market program. It began in 1976 as an experimental project for the Council on the Environment of New York City, with twelve farmers setting up shop in Manhattan under the Queensboro Bridge at Fifty-Ninth Street and Second Avenue, and on part of then crime- and drug-ridden Union Square. Growth has been explosive, with the number of locations rising to twenty-eight in 2002 and some fifty-one outdoor farmers' markets now operating in all five boroughs. Just one of these, the highly popular signature market at Union Square, serves what *New York* magazine describes as "teeming throngs" of eager customers from among the two hundred thousand people a day who pass by on foot. Food stamps are accepted and used, to the delight of officials concerned with the lack of fresh produce at stores in poor neighborhoods and the dominance of fast foods in a city that is outpacing the nation in obesity and its side effects. Over two hundred farmers and fishermen participate in the Greenmarket program, which says it has protected thirty thousand acres of farmland from development. Seventy percent of the participants are Hudson Valley farmers, says city planner and Greenmarket cofounder Barry Benepe. "The program has absolutely saved farming in the Hudson Valley," says an admiring Ann Yonkers, codirector of the successful FreshFarm Markets program in and around Washington, DC.

As much at home in New York City as he is in the upstate town of Saugerties, where he now lives in busy retirement, Benepe claims that getting to know that town inspired him to help launch the Greenmarket idea back in the early 1970s. He saw a rural community that was losing its historical roots as well as its farmland. He knew that New York had a rich history of successful farm markets and in 1976 got foundation support to launch the two pilot projects. It was hard going at first, he says, but sheer persistence has paid off. "I can't tell you the numbers," says Greenmarket cofounder Bob Lewis, an employee of the New York State Department of Agriculture and Markets, "but they would blow your mind."

Lewis claims that the Greenmarket program has generated profound and far-reaching change in how people think. "Greenmarket kicked off the whole local food movement in the U.S. The direct contact between grower and shopper is an entirely different perspective. It's made the farmer a hero, and it's struck a chord in the American psyche. What's happening is amazing. The entire wholesale universe wants local food. We need to scale up to the wholesale level, bring about a new equivalent to what we did in 1976. There's been very progressive change in what supermarkets carry. Colleges all over the country are involved." From my conversations with this irrepressible duo, I gathered no indication that either one is slowing down.

— · —

An indication of how people's relationship to the farmland has changed comes from an unlikely place: the quintessentially suburban Westchester County. To this affluent suburb, in the golden mid-twentieth-century years, there flocked residents many of whom fit the John Cheever mold of classic suburban living: the commuter train, the martinis and cocktail parties, the golf and tennis, and the odd horse or pony. Until recently, few Westchester residents bothered with farming even for the family table. But the revolution of which Bob Lewis speaks has reached Westchester's younger residents, and a classic example is Lisa Schwartz, who with her husband founded and runs Rainbeau Ridge Farms in Bedford Hills. Lisa's sister Karen, a fugitive from the business world, works there, too. The dream began to take shape in 1988, when the Schwartzes bought their "white elephant" house and the 150 acres of poorly tended land on which it stood and began dreaming of restoring the property. "I didn't start farming with a business plan or even a long-term vision," Lisa writes in her book *Over the Rainbeau*. "I just knew I wanted to get closer to nature and my food sources and produce something of value with my own hands."

As spring turned into summer 2011, I visited this farm in the excellent company of Sarah Gould Kagan, daughter of close New York City friends and for many years a Scarsdale resident, and her husband, Stewart. Sarah believes passionately that beneath the stereotypes about Westchester there lurks a vibrant and creative soul that is vividly on display at Rainbeau Ridge. Even though the owner was not around, Sarah along with others there gave me a good sense of how the place works. One garden boasted tidy rows of glistening red leaf lettuce, another featured exuberantly growing eggplant, of which Rainbeau cultivates nine varieties. Multicolored Alpine goats of various sexes and ages, including a frisky swarm of small kids born late in the winter or earlier in the spring, occupied several pens; some were guarded by stalwart llamas positioned to ward off intruding foxes and other predators. Separately penned turkey poults, arrayed along a bar, were squawking loudly. Chickens scurried about. A pet peacock displayed, and so did a tom turkey.

Adult female doe goats had already been milked for the daily cheese-making session. In a separate, meticulously clean shed, several different kinds of chèvre were taking shape under the careful supervision of recent Harvard graduate Blair Harshbarger, a confident woman who aspires to have her own farm one day. Fashioned exclusively from the milk of Rainbeau goats, Lisa's award-winning cheeses are made without the use of citric acid, applied to hasten acidification, which sharpens the taste of commercially made chèvre. A white erase board listed current chores for Ron, one of the farm's few full-time employees. Sample entry: "Check on all problem feet."

Julie, a photographer from Nevada, talked of how, as a novice, only a week after her arrival at Rainbeau, she had been left alone with two very pregnant goats. Assured that nothing would happen, she soon faced the screams of a doe having a difficult birth. Julie got on the phone with her father, a veterinarian who, when parts of a baby began to emerge, advised her to pull hard, *out* and *down*. She followed instructions and finally, with help from the weary mother goat, succeeded in delivering the record-size baby of the birthing season, an eight pounder. "There was no time to be afraid," she said. "I simply had to keep on going."

Rainbeau educates all sorts of people. "Roots," "Buds," and "Sprouts" —elementary schoolchildren from Westchester and Connecticut—come after school to plant, harvest, cook, eat, and work with the goats and other farm animals. At home one mom told author Holly Tarson that kids enrolled in the program "will eat almost any vegetable. They are willing to try it because they've grown it or they've seen it grown." Teenage apprentices undertake more complex tasks, some of them volunteering their time in return for food. Adults attend cooking classes: Lisa Schwartz's book *Over the Rainbeau* not only tells the story of the Schwartzes and their farm; it is also a cookbook offering advice on using the farmstead products. It all seems to go well beyond the joys and thrills of life on the farm, she seems to be saying. It's also about teaching people the benefits, in the community as well as in the home, of living sustainably. Without meeting the lady, I left mighty impressed by those convictions—and by her obviously successful conversion of what had been a conventional country estate, complete with swimming pool, into a rewarding if challenging business.

Backing up individual family efforts is an infrastructure of support and protection for Westchester farming. "Agriculture! Westchester County's Best Kept Secret," trumpets a brochure published by the county government's Agriculture and Farmland Protection Board (AFPB), which goes on to outline the economic, environmental, and cultural virtues of maintaining a healthy agriculture industry. Also highlighted is farming's role in protecting drinking water supplies for Westchester and other New York metropolitan area residents: Rainwater falling onto Westchester farmland percolates gently into the ground, filtering pollutants en route to the Croton reservoir system.

The AFPB was founded in 2000 to "maintain the economic viability, environmental and landscape preservation values associated with agriculture." In 2001 the AFPB established a county Agricultural District, a designation under state law that offers farmers fiscal and other benefits. In 2004 it followed up with a comprehensive, carefully considered plan to protect the county's farms and farmers. Implementation continues.

On the private side, the Westchester Land Trust, founded in 2000 and starting from a low base, has been successful in gaining ground for open space and recreational land, increasing tenfold the number of protected acres in over a decade of activity. A recent innovation is a Farmer Match program that links farmers who need land with landowners willing to have their land farmed. With little fanfare, a Farmers Network that the trust created has attracted a diverse assortment of citizens "interested in making local agriculture more sustainable."

To be sure, Westchester's affluence distorts its farming scene. Few could afford to create the Stone Barns Center for Food and Agriculture in Pocantico Hills, a beautiful education and community resource that has been lavishly supported by the Rockefeller family. John D. Rockefeller Jr. built the Normandy-style barns on the family's Pocantico Hills estate in the 1920s for use as a dairy farm. Later they fell into disuse and remained dormant until Peggy Dulany, one of David Rockefeller's daughters, arrived on the scene. She proposed to her father that the barns be restored and opened to the public in honor of her late mother, also named Peggy, who was avidly interested in gardening and farming.

The renovation of the handsome buildings was completed, and the reborn site made its debut in 2004. Its amenities include 4.5 acres of tidy organic vegetable garden, a boutique farmers' market, education programs, a well-stocked gift shop, and the highly regarded Blue Hill restaurant, which has no menu and serves only food seasonally available from local sources. When I visited, the tours were booked solid—one hundred thousand people a year visit the barns—and the pathways were teeming with visitors, especially young families. My tour guide burbled with enthusiasm about the many varieties of food she showed us. In the manner of Julia Child, her most frequently used adjective was "delicious."

Some of Westchester's farms fall into the vanity category or serve as toys for the horsey set. The overall count of active farms in the county has continued to drop, though at a less precipitous rate than in the 1990s. "No one knows how to make this truly financially viable," cautions Lisa Schwartz, who does not need to earn her living from Rainbeau Ridge. Still, says county environmental planner David Kvinge, the number of Westchester farmers treating their operations as a serious business is on a rapid upswing, with new ideas and projects bubbling up frequently. "It's been really, really exciting to watch," he says.

For all the new fervor about farming, and for all the talk about its economic and environmental benefits for Hudsonians, state support for farmland protection has a checkered history and a cloudy present. In the aftermath of the great wave of state and federal environmental legislation of the 1970s, it became clear that new sources of funding for local jurisdictions were needed for them to comply with the new demands for toxic cleanups, clean water, and clean air. New York State voters approved an environmental bond act in 1986 but in 1990 narrowly turned down a larger one; it was the only one of eleven such measures dating back to 1910 that the state's voters had ever rejected. In 1992, consequently, then governor Mario Cuomo established the

Environmental Protection Fund to support capital projects to protect and preserve the state's natural heritage. It would mostly be under-written on a pay-as-you-go basis out of revenues from a real estate transfer tax. Among the beneficiaries of funds from this source would be measures to control agricultural nonpoint pollution sources, con-serve soil and water, and protect farmlands via purchases of develop-ment rights.

This fund played a key role in the successful outcome of the Sterling Forest struggle when then governor George Pataki conjured up $16 million in EPF funds at a key moment. But not even he could prevent others in Albany from treating the EPF as an easy score, a place to find earmarked funds to siphon into the general account during tough eco-nomic times. According to state comptroller DiNapoli, EPF appropria-tions had been diverted in this manner in seven out of the eight most recent state budgets. DiNapoli has complained relatively politely about bureaucratic delays in getting funds from the program into the hands of needy farmers and the resulting backlog of authorized but undisbursed cash in EPF accounts. Then, reported DiNapoli in 2010: "This cash has frequently been reprogrammed to fill General Fund deficits caused by unsustainable State budget practices where recurring spending exceeds recurring revenue. A total of $854 million—39 percent of EPF appro-priations—has been swept to the General Fund." Results for the pro-gram's farmland protection component have been equally disturbing: only $95.5 million spent out of $205.6 million allocated.

Tied Up in Knots banners a forcefully stated report from a private Albany watchdog agency called Environmental Advocates of New York. Subtitled "How Red Tape, Executive Meddling & Staff Shortages Are Strangling New York's Environmental Protection Fund," the report charges Albany with a "Byzantine, unnecessarily complicated and inef-ficient process" to get remaining EPF funds in the pipeline, sometimes stretching as long as four or five years, and at last disbursed. Approvals must often come from as many as five state agencies with sharply divergent agendas. With only two full-time people on the staff, the fund has only managed to preserve thirty-six thousand acres of farmland versus more than four hundred thousand acres under a similar program in Pennsylvania, where staff members' workload is far lighter. DiNapoli notes that from 2000 to 2010 there has been a net increase in the number of farms in the neighbor states of Pennsylvania, Connecticut, New Jersey, and Massachusetts, all with the largest historical outlays for farmland protection.

The state and private interests alike are given poor marks for not being more effective in helping farmers' market the region or their brands and their goods. For all the good foods and wines produced along the Hudson, the region has yet to come up with a local counterpart to the Idaho potato, the Vidalia onion, Northern California's Napa Valley wines, or Maryland's blue crabs. Says Benepe: "The state should put out a Request for Proposals to market the Hudson Valley. The branding efforts up to now have just not been successful."

"New York State just hasn't figured out how to make a business case for it," argues Lisa Schwartz of Rainbeau Ridge. "They've relinquished the opportunity to brand the Hudson Valley. It's all very tricky right now." She points out the bureaucratic delays besetting the state's Purchase of Development Rights and other programs where cumbersome rules and regulations stand in the way and notes the lack of public water supplies. "I'm optimistic in a generic sense," she concludes. "But on the ground there's a long way to go." One hopeful sign is that, with little help from Albany, Hudson farmers are banding together to market Hudson cider from the region's ample supply of high-quality apples.

Despite Albany's lackluster performance and the myriad other obstacles that practitioners face, it may be that the decline of Hudson

Valley farming has bottomed out and that a modest resurgence of small-scale farming is in progress. The American Farmland Trust's Don Buckloh sees signs of an uptick, and so does Seth McKee, Scenic Hudson's land conservation director. While the average age of surviving farmers in the region is a hefty fifty-seven, the most recent Agricultural Census also showed an encouraging 49 percent increase in the number of young farmers age twenty-five or less. Many such people are learning how to eke a sustainable living from very small landholdings.

The Open Space Institute is especially hopeful about the four-county Catskills region. In 2011 OSI reported that the 2.7-million-acre region contains 520,000 acres "where development can occur without direct impact to open space resources. Given 140,000 acres of land are currently developed, we conclude that the region could hypothetically quadruple development before directly developing the open space resources." Another recent OSI study, entitled *Ground Up*, compares food production in the Catskills' Sullivan County with demand in the New York metropolitan area for locally produced foodstuffs, concluding that the region "has the potential to produce enough healthy, locally grown food to feed millions of people in New York City and beyond."

Researchers from Columbia University's Urban Design Center have found data confirming that farming in the county had bottomed out, with 235 remaining farms in 2003 and an increase of 149 farms by 2008. The study includes six case studies showing heavy farmer reliance on New York City's Greenmarkets program and on high-end restaurants with whose chefs they deal directly. With more than half the county's productive land not being used for agriculture and overall regional demand for local food far exceeding supply, the study concludes, Sullivan County "has the land, water, location, and potential connections to become a premier food supply source for the New York City metropolitan area" and a "vibrant sector" in its economy.

Credit for what may be a positive trend for the longer term must go to innovative programs such as Glynwood and Greenmarket, to New York City's hordes of eager farm market customers, and to the spread of interest beyond the city in locally produced and organic food. Said Holly Tarson in an *Edible Hudson Valley* article: "It's farmland that preserves our rolling hills green with crops and open space, free from overdevelopment. Whatever you love about life in the Valley, chances are you owe it to the farmers." In the words of a 2004 study commissioned by the American Farmland Trust, "Agriculture in the Hudson River Valley has consistently demonstrated its health through the resiliency and adaptive behavior of its entrepreneurs in the face of real challenges."

CHAPTER 9

For the Sport of It

FROM THE FIRST TEE OF THE CHALLENGING GARRISON GOLF CLUB, high in the Highlands, on a crisp, clear early autumn day, you look out north and west at a magnificent panorama, with the Hudson's Narrows and Storm King Mountain front and center. Then in stages you descend through groves of trees, artfully sited water swales, old colonial-era stone walls, and pathways scattered in the woods. You complete your round, bemoaning the number of golf balls lost, then review it over an excellent meal at the Garrison's Valley restaurant, said by some to be the best in Putnam County. Later you enjoy a massage or join a yoga class, then retire to a comfortable bedroom on the grounds. The room is one of four that constitute the first stage of what the property's owners think of as an "executive build-out"—a small sixty-room hotel that would maintain the Highlands' distinctive cultural character while also enabling visitors to spend a pleasant night with a great view up and across the river. The following day you try the Garrison's links a second time, shooing away the Canada geese wandering the fairways, and return home with pleasant memories of a weekend well spent.

"This is the worst investment I ever made," moans the Garrison's owner Chris Davis, a keen environmentalist. "Golf is a terrible business. So seasonal." Yet he is far from alone in placing his bets on a sports-crazed Hudson Valley, where outdoor recreation has become another major driver of the new regional economy. The Garrison was once a haven called Bill Brown's Fitness Farm, designed for boxing aficionados. Kayaking, fishing the Hudson and world-class streams and tributaries, hiking and biking, rock climbing, cross-country skiing, and yes, even swimming in the Hudson's long-fetid waters are all sports that have become popular in the region.

In the mid-1970s, when my family and I started weekending in Cornwall, I would occasionally venture out onto the still-dirty river aboard a battered aluminum canoe or as crew for a friend who had a speedy but temperamental Star sailboat that he kept near the Newburgh–Beacon Bridge. For a while I captained a peculiar, trailerable Dovekie sailboat I called the *Mudhen* that you could either sail or row in the manner of a Roman galley slave—hidden below a rounded deck, oars extended from portholes. From a small launching facility at Cornwall Landing, I would set forth onto Newburgh Bay.

Cornwall had a small, standoffish yacht club, and a few military people kept small boats moored at West Point. Transient sailors picked up moorings at Manhattan's Seventy-Ninth Street Boat Basin and spent bouncy nights there. You could book an afternoon or daylong cruise aboard a sprightly little historical motor vessel called the *Commander*, built in 1917 and still plying Hudson Highlands waters. For those of us who ventured forth onto the river during those times, the thought of swimming in it simply never came to mind. Hudson steamers such as the famed *Mary Powell* had long since vanished, and the *Clearwater* was barely launched. So we had its beauties and shortcomings pretty much to ourselves.

No longer so. In the summer of 2009, reporter Corey Kilgannon undertook a sixty-hour Hudson boating journey that caught the flavor of the variety and stimulation accompanying the region's reconnection with its waters. Kilgannon boarded a friend's fifteen-foot kayak in Lower Manhattan and paddled upriver, past the aircraft carrier *Intrepid*, to a rendezvous near the island's northern tip with Captain Chip Reynolds's 1989 replica of Henry Hudson's three-masted *Half Moon*. Hauled aboard for the night, Kilgannon later experienced a series of adventures that included hitchhiking rides aboard a "sporty white jet-boat," an inflatable Sea Tow rescue vessel, and a Catskill-based twin-diesel power yacht that at full speed burns 48 gallons of fuel an hour.

Enroute, Kilgannon sighted portions of the river "filled by tugboats, tankers, Jet Skiers, and recreational boaters towing large inner tubes." He joined wine tasters at a waterside restaurant in Newburgh; saw beaches "with canoes or kayaks pulled up and people swimming"; Rascal's Riverdogs, a floating hot dog stand at the mouth of Catskill Creek; and a "green" watercraft that sometimes functioned under biodiesel, wind, and solar power. In sum, said Kilgannon, echoing my own experience, the voyage revealed a world to him that "bears no resemblance to the Hudson I knew down around New York City."

The words of Tom Fox, a water taxi operator in New York City, catch the flavor of how boaters have come to treasure the river. "It's an incredible resource for the region," he told filmmaker Josh Aronson in his PBS documentary *Hudson Valley Stories*. "I want to reconnect my passengers with the river. I want them to understand this river, share the love for it that I feel. You can only do that if you get out on it. Get them out on the water; they will be better stewards of the river. I firmly believe that the river is just beginning to be explored." Fox yearns for the time, a century ago, when the river was "cheek by jowl" with watercraft. And he firmly believes, "That day will come again."

For all the hazards that paddlers face from tricky winds and swirling currents, kayaking remains the most frequently cited symbol for the revival of boat traffic along the river. A leading advocate is Scenic

Hudson's Ned Sullivan, who promotes getting out on the water as "the most exciting way to experience the Hudson" and paddling a kayak as "the 'greenest' and healthiest way of doing this." Online during the summer of 2009, Sullivan reported having been a volunteer monitor escorting two hundred swimmers crossing Newburgh Bay, on a "gorgeous" summer Saturday, to raise funds for the *Clearwater*. He had been enchanted, he reported, "by how different the world looks from the middle of a river or lake, not to mention the access kayaks provide to secluded spots—such as wetlands and islands—impossible for landlubbers to reach. The feeling of escape and discovery when exploring places like these is almost palpable."

New York State's Hudson River Valley Greenway organization, which encourages planners to think regionally rather than locally, supports kayak enthusiasts by promoting its Hudson River Greenway Water Trail with information about launch sites and rest stops along a 150-mile route ending in New York Harbor. Each summer the Greenway sponsors a Great Hudson River Paddle, from Manhattan to Albany, that attracts hundreds of participants.

Hudson boaters less adventuresome than the paddlers, such as Mary Armao and Kevin McCarthy, can charter the Troy-based MV *Rensselaer*, a forty-foot Dutch-style canal boat, and make their own way downriver to Manhattan. Without the benefit of any prior boating experience, the McCarthys reported in *BoatU.S.* magazine, they responded to an ad advising them that none was necessary and cast off unaccompanied. They successfully cruised the Highlands region, mastering the arts of docking (usually for free), anchoring, and navigating the river's shoals. They studied the region's past, visiting Olana and the Hudson River Maritime Museum on Kingston's waterfront, as well as a seventeenth-century historical site, Staat House, that is still occupied by the family that built it. So captivated by all this were the McCarthys that, they said in their article, "we knew in our hearts that more cruising, and even boat ownership, was in our future."

The Web lists several companies that offer similar bare-boat charters on Hudson waters. For sailors the New York Yacht Club hosts an annual group cruise. And each October, at the height of the fall foliage season, American Cruise Lines offers eight-day, seven-night runs upriver that it describes as "small ship cruising done perfectly" aboard comfortable vessels sleeping no more than 120 people.

Colder weather brings new recreational opportunities. An excess population of white-tailed deer gives hunters plenty to shoot at on brisk autumn days. Sometimes in December the ponds freeze before the snow comes, and chances pop up to skate or play ice hockey on "black ice" in such places as the Black Rock Forest. Opportunities for cross-country and downhill skiing, snowshoeing, and snowmobiling are seldom far away. Every so often, the river itself freezes hard enough for intrepid iceboaters to coax their old rigs out from barns in towns such as Tivoli or Germantown and head for the river. On display at the Hudson River Maritime Museum in Kingston are several of these rickety but speedy craft, which can race along at sixty miles per hour or more when conditions are right. The museum also offers films giving you a taste of the thrills and hazards of a traditional Hudson sport much diminished by changing weather patterns. Crashes are frequent, but zealots report a splendid camaraderie when things go wrong.

Along the river's steep banks in the Highlands, and scattered through the valley, are excellent facilities belonging to New York State's impressive array of 178 parks and preserves, the latter given a special mandate to protect wildlife as well as provide for human recreation. The system is "still the best in the country" despite recent budget woes, claimed

New York's environmental protection commissioner Joe Martens, a firm believer in their economic importance as well as in the joys of just being out there. Within the valley there is no better example of the system's beauties and benefits than the string of protected areas along the eighty-five-thousand-acre Shawangunk Ridge, a fifty-mile northern extension of the Appalachians to which twenty million Americans have easy access.

Formerly a band of lightly used wilderness and farmland, now about half safeguarded from random development, the Shawangunks (pronounced SHAWN-gunks) are now visited by almost half a million hikers, mountain bikers, and rock climbers a year. From an extensive network of trails and restored carriage roads, visitors enjoy panoramic views of the Catskills and the Hudson Highlands. Closer by are dramatic vertical white-rock cliffs up to nine hundred feet in height and crystal-clear lakes, ponds, and streams.

"It's the most visually stunning place in the state," says Shawangunks enthusiast Robert Anderberg. A former park ranger there, he then went to law school and joined the Open Space Institute. He now serves as its senior vice president and general counsel and from that bully pulpit has single-handedly brought more than twenty-five thousand acres of this paradise under protection. "People fall in love with this resource," he adds. The details of the romance offer you a sense of what these places can do for your soul—and for the area's pocketbook.

Here one can best appreciate the Hudson Valley's vaunted biological diversity. Though only 12 percent of New York State's land, the valley is home to 85 percent of all its species of plants and animals, including some two hundred species of birds and an impressive array of other wild creatures. To be found in the Shawangunks are timber rattlesnakes and black bears, as well as such charismatic species as the fast-diving peregrine falcon and a rarely seen but robust population of weasel-like mammals called fishers. Much of the preserve's northern section lies in backcountry, where the only trails are those made by animals.

One night in 1987 local teenager Joseph David Helt and three friends drove into these wildlands. Their Subaru got stuck in a ditch, and they were not able to move it. As a major snowstorm moved in, Helt began a five-mile walk back down to the town of Ellenville to get help. Despite repeated search efforts, he was never seen again and his corpse was never found.

Within the Minnewaska State Park Preserve, near the town of Gardiner, hikers and bikers and cross-country skiers can choose between lovingly restored carriage roads, forming boundaries between wildlands and human settlements, and blazed foot trails leading to Hudson and Catskill vistas that the Shawangunk Ridge Coalition describes as "simply breathtaking." Cliffs almost completely surround crystal-clear lakes nestled in basins where the swimming is idyllic. The Shawangunk State Park Preserve especially recommends Lake Awosting, where hikers can approach a "pleasing" rock slab beach above which are "a number of overlooks that give them a fantastic view of the dancing waves below." Waterfalls cascade. This preserve, encompassing more than twenty-two thousand acres in the Shawangunks, is New York State's third largest park.

Added to the Minnewaska preserve in 2007, thanks to the Open Space Institute, was the second of the Shawangunks' three crown jewels: the fifty-four-hundred-acre Sam's Point Preserve near the town of Ellenville at the southern end of the Shawangunks. Listed by the Nature Conservancy as one of its "last great places on earth," Sam's Point features deep caves holding up to eight or ten feet of snow well into the summer. Rare dwarf pitch pines growing out of the bedrock thrill botanizers. "Nature Conservancy people go nuts about these ecological treasures," says Anderberg.

A third eighty-five-hundred-acre section of the ridge called the Mohonk Preserve lies a short drive westward from the bustling university town of New Paltz and a mere ninety miles from New York City. Established by the Smiley family, owners of the Mohonk Mountain House (see below), in 1963, this is the state's largest private nonprofit nature preserve, a carefully managed landscape connected by seventy-five miles of carriage roads to Minnewaska State Park Preserve and other portions of the Shawangunk range. Originally encompassing five thousand acres, the preserve has grown in size to eighty-five hundred acres, once again thanks largely to the Open Space Institute. It has tirelessly engaged in deal making in the region, having concluded more than one hundred separate transactions with local landowners. Voluntarily rather than by eminent domain, they have committed their properties to protection by means of outright purchases, easements, or acquisition of development rights. The busy Mohonk Preserve has thirteen thousand dues-paying members and 370 community volunteers. More than one hundred thousand students a year, as well as scientists doing field research, participate in using, studying, and maintaining this place.

Within the Mohonk Preserve, the hole in the doughnut, lies the Mohonk Mountain House, a nationally registered historical landmark that sits high on the cliffs, overlooking yet another glistening lake. Founded as a modest guesthouse in 1869 by Alfred H. Smiley, who had discovered the place while on a picnic, the Mohonk lodge gradually developed into a large hotel with accommodations for up to five hundred people and its own twenty-two-hundred-acre stretch of parkland. For a long while it remained austere and dry in the hands of Smiley and his twin brother, Albert K. Smiley, both Quakers. Now juiced up for modern guests with new amenities, including a spa, the lodge offers a wide range of recreational activities, from snow tubing to fly fishing, carriage and horseback rides, and golf. Reviewers generally love it, though the food gets mixed marks. The Smiley clan amassed both the Mohonk properties, spinning off the Mohonk Preserve as a separate, privately and well-managed entity in 1963.

At the epicenter of sports fans' love affair with the Shawangunks lies a series of world-famous grayish cliffs in the Mohonk Preserve called the Trapps, where rock climbers—as many as five hundred a day during peak seasons and ten thousand a year—gather to test their skills against the vertical walls. During the late 1930s a tireless German mountaineer, Fritz Miessner, discovered and explored these cliffs and began to climb them. After a hiatus during World War II and well beyond, usage remained restricted to small numbers of climbers, almost all members of the Appalachian Mountain Club, who tried to set and maintain safety standards as traffic gradually grew.

The sport took off like a rocket in the 1960s and has steadily expanded in recent years, with increasing numbers of climbers from all over coming to the region to test untried routes (called "problems") and use techniques that include unprotected free ascents and safer "top-roping"—climbing a cliff with a rope always anchored above. Today, says the New Paltz Chamber of Commerce, the "Gunks," with twelve hundred documented climbing routes, are rock climbers' "single busiest destination in North America." Parking lots fill early in the day, despite the reality that, as one of the guidebooks flatly puts it, "rock climbing and any variation of this sport are dangerous; whether you're a novice or an expert, you can be seriously injured or KILLED." In an effort to understand a small fraction of the mystique and dangers of this bracing sport, I spent the better part of a balmy April day on the Underhill carriage road at the foot of the cliff. With me were Bob Anderberg and a part-time ranger working for the preserve.

The "Gunks," my hosts explained, rank with Yosemite and the Tetons as a top challenge for climbers from all over the country and the world. Shaped by the collision of two tectonic plates, with accompanying folding and faulting, the sheer escarpment was then smoothed by glaciations during the Pleistocene ice age of ten thousand years ago. Its sedimentary rock, called quartz conglomerate, has just the right consistency for climbers to attach their elaborate gear—not too crumbly or slippery. We sauntered along the carriage road, looking across scattered arrays of boulders called talus at the foot of the cliffs where climbers were working. Nearly every inch of this landscape is carefully documented in the literature, each climb equipped with a name, such as Enduro Man, Tequila Mockingbird, or Snooky's Return.

Understanding the instruction-manual lingo does not come easy. *The Climber's Guide to the Shawangunks*, for example, recommends a route called Ruby Saturday as "a really good climb with exciting moves." After you somehow get off the ground, you are advised to "climb straight up the face about 12 feet till standing on a horizontal, step right and up to a thin horizontal (V1). Step left and crank/dyno up to a small left-pointing flake at base of short left-facing corner (crux). Move up to wide crack (10 Metolius or 5 Friend helpful). Then up face to belay on ledge below, first overhangs near right-facing flakes (80 ft.)."

We watched as climbers above us followed such instructions. A young novice close by tried vainly to follow suggestions from partners holding her ropes and encouraging her to move her hands and feet upward and sideways in tiny, carefully choreographed stages marked with color-coded ribbons attached to the wall. Eventually, after watching her struggle for some time, we left her immobile, clinging forlornly to the cliff, eyes cast longingly downward, some ten feet up. Later I spotted her on the road she had somehow managed to get back down to. She was actually smiling.

A number of the climbers were festooned with little devices called carabiners or quickdraws, ropes, cams, and other climbing bric-a-brac.

Some also carried rubber mattresses on their backs. I asked about these and learned that they are used in a variation of rock climbing called "bouldering." Here the goal is to conquer not an entire cliff several hundred feet high but a single boulder equipped with what are classified as "problems," such as having to work oneself out from underneath an overhanging face. I watched in awe as several teenagers attacked such a boulder. You place the mat. Then you briefly hang on to the underside before making a giant effort to swing upwards, holding on with little more than fingernails, catch your feet on something, and then swing up and free. I saw no successes at this game. Sometimes the climber miraculously manages to gather strength and successfully leap to the next little handhold. What far more often happens is that the fly on the wall hangs there for a while, then loses strength and drops off onto the mat.

In an effort to learn more about rock climbing as a sport, I attended an introductory, hands-on lesson on the subject. Early on a Sunday morning, I ventured forth aboard the District of Columbia Metrorail's Red Line subway and debarked near the end of the line at Rockville Center, on whose broad thoroughfares hardly a pedestrian was to be seen. A brisk walk along these empty streets soon had me within sight of a cavernous Marlo furniture store, in one corner of which a modest doorway marked the entrance to the Earth Treks Indoor Climbing Center. Inside, vertical walls up to forty feet in height accommodated climbers of all ages, mostly teenagers and younger kids but also attracting an encouraging number of older people.

The decibel level was high, with climbers yelling commands to ground-level belayers minding carefully anchored climbing ropes attached for safety to harnesses buckled to thighs and midriffs. "*Belay on!*," "*Climb on!*," "*Gotcha!*," "*Lowering!*" commands added to the din. Instructors were monitoring the student climbers from positions along the padded gym floors, advising novices to "maintain a relaxed state of mind" and rely principally on legs, not arms, to "travel vertically." Attached to the wall were handholds and footholds, each marked with a color-coded and numbered ribbon advising the climber of the route's difficulty. From time to time a climber, having scrambled upward and reached the summit, would advise the belayer to feed out some rope to allow him or her to rappel down the wall, periodically kicking free of it out into open space, and return to ground level.

Never having climbed anything even so little as a tall ladder without experiencing a certain tingling of apprehension in my toes, I had expected to do nothing more than learn basic belaying procedure and act as belayer during my three-hour Introduction to Rock Climbing class. I did put on a pair of climbing shoes, pinched at the toes to stack them up and increase foot power. Our beginner group, about twenty strong, gathered in a circle facing sinewy instructors Dean and Cynthia, who split us up into teams of two or three, then patiently showed us how to buckle up our harnesses, tie in a climbing rope using a double-figure-eight knot, set up the belay with the help of a device called a carabiner, and review safety procedures. Then they did a brief demo run, with Dean belaying and Cynthia tidily poised on the wall and moving effortlessly sideways and upward. Then, calmly, Dean handed me the climbing rope and said, "Go on up."

Being about triple the age of the next oldest person in the group, I briefly considered turning him down and deferring to the younger set. But then came the feeling of not wanting to disappoint my belaying teammates, a sense of pride, and the consolation of improved upper-body strength, thanks to weekly gym workouts in recent years. "*Climb on!*" and "*Up rope!*" I sang out to belayer Brendan, trying to hide my malaise, then reached out for the lowest sets of hand- and footholds fastened to the wall. Some were hollowed enough to get four fingers securely into, others were merely slightly pocked mounds. "Keep your center of gravity close to the wall," advised Dean. "Use your toes, not your whole foot. Keep your arms straight."

So up I clambered, moving slowly, feeling ever stronger and more confident, careful not to look down at the floor receding beneath me and satisfied that the security of the belaying rope would keep me from falling. I reached an overhang about twenty feet up, where the angle of the wall exceeded ninety degrees, and decided this was enough. "Slack," I signaled Brendan, and I rappelled back down the wall, reaching the ground quickly. I had achieved a clean ascent with no falls and came away pleased with myself.

I thought back to a vivid time in 1957. I was in the final stages of naval flight school in Corpus Christi, nearing the moment when I would earn my coveted wings. Along with other trainees in my class, after many hours of painstaking instruction, I had been deemed ready to strap myself into a very powerful and tricky single-seat, single-engine airplane called an AD Skyraider that I had never flown before. I was to wrestle the thing into the air, circle the field, and then somehow get back to earth with no help other than occasional radioed words of encouragement from an instructor on the ground. In the ready room he had briefed our group one last time, then said, "Okay, guys, go take a nervous leak, and then go out there and fly that sucker."

I taxied gingerly out to the runway, took off as advised by the manual, circled around, and somehow landed. Thrilled, adrenaline pumping, I could not wait to do it all again. And so it was with climbing the wall. After my descent I quickly had another go at it and was soon scrambling past that overhang to the full height of the wall, looking neither down nor back. Again, I scored a clean ascent. Back down, I watched, with newly found scorn, as a pudgy older woman struggled up the wall, huffing and puffing. In a little way I had come to sense the appeal of this burgeoning sport and understand in a minor way why so many people would choose to come in out of a sunny spring day and spend much of it in a sweaty gym grappling with a vertical artificial wall.

"How did you like it?" asked a fellow climber, photographer Jay Mallin, as we waited for the Red Line train home. Mallin, who as it turned out is the son of an old *Time* magazine colleague of mine, was carrying both a skateboard and a bag full of climbing gear. He said that he tries to get out to the Earth Treks gym once a week to hone his skills in preparation for the several times a year that he goes off with climbing buddies to outdoor sites all over. He often visits the Shawangunks, for which he expresses particular admiration. "The climbing is great and the views are magnificent," he said. "I go up there as much as I can." When his group cannot find an available campsite, they head for a bed-and-breakfast or a motel.

What is the overall economic effect of recreation in the Shawangunks? Without even counting the jobs and revenues stemming from the Mohonk Mountain House, researchers from a firm called Business Opportunities were able to rate the three parks, almost totally unvisited as recently as the 1970s, as having had "a significant impact on the local economy of the region." After careful study the research team found it "reasonable" to conclude that annually 362,659 people visit, spending $13,051,000 and generating $459,000 in local sales taxes. The parks, moreover, supported 358 jobs, most of which were underwritten not out of operations or capital budgets but by visitor spending.

These figures compare favorably with ones offered by the developer of the proposed "Seven Peaks" project in the nearby town of Mamakating, which a spokesman described as "a low-density, legacy second-home enclave." His company would straddle the ridge, putting forty-nine units on the 653-acre site along with a luxury hotel. At a recent public hearing to review the project, citizens raised many objections. Only a few expressed enthusiasm for the most commonly stated virtues of such projects: the jobs and tax revenues it would create. Village of Ellenville mayor Jeffrey Kaplan said he was "ecstatic" over the addition of Sam's Point to the Minnewaska park, indicating a preference for preserving wildlife habitat and recreational opportunities over the customary alternatives of high-end homes and golf courses.

Private property owners, environmental groups, and a few state agencies are striving to maintain the values that support sports. Scenic Hudson and the Open Space Institute, with broad support from other groups, continue their efforts to sequester land for outdoor recreation and add it to the state's already extensive state parks system. Early in 2011, advocates of open space preservation were keenly looking toward Albany for new support for the parks after the deeply disappointing performance of Governor David Paterson, who in 2010 had for budget reasons tried to shut down most of them. This move was not popular.

Part III:
Politics and Principles

CHAPTER 10

The Gotham Model

ON DECEMBER 16, 1973, A TAR-LADEN DUMP TRUCK ON A MISSION to fill potholes along a portion of New York City's decrepit, elevated West Side Highway caused a section of it, in the meatpacking district near downtown Gansevoort Street, to collapse. A sixty-foot stretch of the antique cobblestone road, which connected Lower Manhattan with the Midtown Hudson River piers and the Henry Hudson Parkway leading uptown to the George Washington Bridge, was left in a shambles. The vehicle lay "upended like a turtle on its back," wrote essayist Phillip Lopate, its driver badly wounded.

Notable about the event was not just the negligence leading to the highway's often-forewarned demise. It also set off a turbulent but ultimately productive quarter century of planning and rebuilding that resulted not just in a restored roadway but also in the imaginative 550-acre Hudson River Park. It is Manhattan's largest park project since Central Park was completed in 1873 and is widely said to have had an equally powerful effect on the overall structure of the city.

Restored, reconnected to adjacent communities, are five miles of Lower Manhattan's long-lost Hudson shoreline from Battery Park City near Ground Zero to Fifty-Ninth Street. The park plan caters to the needs or hopes of those straightforwardly in search of a fixed-up highway and commercial opportunities. It also responds to recreational and cultural values and to the requirements of striped bass and other migratory fish species. Beneficiaries are pedestrians, in-line skaters, bikers, paddlers, sunbathers, moviegoers, and nature and sports lovers, including fishermen. Motorists' priorities, about which not many New Yorkers are deeply concerned, are also adequately served. In combination with the brilliantly designed, landscaped, and illuminated High Line a short distance eastward and the prominent Whitney Museum's decision to relocate at its foot, Manhattan's Lower West Side with its newly reforged links to the Hudson shore offers what the fiery urbanist Jane Jacobs called the "ghost towns" upstream a powerful model for guidance.

Power broker Robert Moses, to some a villain and to others a genius, had for many years cleverly used his enormous reservoir of political clout to ram a network of express highways though the city and adjacent suburbs. But he was not a major player in the protracted struggle over how to replace the West Side Highway. Nor was the impassioned Jacobs, who had spent a lifetime in opposition to "urban renewal" initiatives that destroyed poor but resilient communities, manning the barricades this time. Moses was long since out of power, and Jacobs, though peripherally involved, had fled Manhattan for Toronto.

But even without their direct involvement, the thoughts of those fierce warriors did much to frame the long and often bitter debate about how to reconfigure the roadway and adjacent spaces. Regardless of the deeper merits or shortcomings of rival proposals, they came to be measured mostly by how likely they seemed to fatten the pockets of vested interests or, alternatively, respond to values promoted by community activists, environmental leaders, and liberal pundits.

In 1973 there was little need to consider rebuilding the West Side Highway, though this was the option that Moses quietly favored. With construction starting in 1927, it was the nation's first elevated highway. It was designed to launch motorists on an almost traffic-free trip nearly as far north as Poughkeepsie and to separate autos in transit from the crime-ridden hurly-burly of local ocean freight and passenger traffic tying up the cobblestone streets below. But the shift in container shipping toward new facilities across the harbor in New Jersey and the falloff of the ocean liner business subsequently caused the sharp decline of those once-bustling piers and adjacent blocks with their rough stevedore culture.

They had, said Jacobs in her classic book *The Death and Life of Great American Cities,* become part of a Lower Manhattan "ring of stagnation, decay, vacancies and vestigial industries." But life crept on. "In and among the decaying piers," reported the New York State Development Project, "wherever they could reach the water, people attempted to find places to sit, walk, jog, and bike. The area was hardly adequate for public recreation. It was not maintained for public use, and some areas were actually unsafe—but people came nonetheless." What was left of the elevated highway, which remained untouched for many years, became popular among joggers and bikers.

"My friends and I took in many a pier concert from that highway," said writer Jeff Saltzman. "It was a great place to hang out and gave great views of the concerts below."

So the way was open for the city to consider not putting the West Side Highway back up at vast cost but instead tearing it down and fashioning a far less expensive and more people-friendly replacement at or below grade. While pondering various options, the city created a temporary north-south roadway along the Twelfth Avenue/West Street waterfront, along which traffic flowed surprisingly smoothly.

Prolonged discussions about the shape and dimensions of a new roadway culminated in a consensus favoring what became known as Westway, a massive two billion dollar or more scheme. In one early version the plan involved creating some 169 acres of offshore landfill through which most of a six-lane, 4.2-mile road would tunnel. "New" land above the tube, as well as some parkland along the shore, would be allocated to businesses, residences, and parks, and $1.7 billion in federal funds from the interstate highway system would largely underwrite this complex, whose centerpiece would be what would become Interstate Highway 478.

Political support for Westway arrived in large quantities. Advocacy came from President Ronald Reagan as well as from ex-presidents Gerald Ford and Jimmy Carter, New York State governor Nelson Rockefeller, New York City mayor John Lindsay, and a bevy of other local officials. David Rockefeller and other downtown bankers were quick to jump aboard, as were real estate interests and labor leaders, including an unaccustomed bedfellow: the AFL/CIO's powerful Harry Van Arsdale. Architecture critics Ada Louise Huxtable, Paul Goldberger, and Peter Blake applauded, the latter calling the plan "ingenious" and the result of "visionary" thinking.

By 1982 it seemed highly likely that Westway would win a steady green light. But then there surfaced a wave of opposition from the same sectors that had long opposed Robert Moses–style disfigurement of traditional neighborhoods, as evidenced by the infamous Lower Manhattan Expressway and the proposed bifurcation of beloved Washington Square at the southern end of Fifth Avenue. Journalist and urban critic Roberta Brandes Gratz dismissed the Westway plan as a "crazed multi-billion dollar city-in-the river landfill." Marcy Benstock, director of the New York Clean Air Campaign, argued strongly about air pollution consequences. The tireless attorney Albert Butzel, representing the Sierra Club, applied to the lower Hudson the knowledge he had gained upriver from his successful prior involvement in the Storm King Mountain dispute. In Manhattan he led a team of lawyers once again arguing in federal courts about the harm the Westway dredging and landfilling would do to striped bass and other species of migratory fish using the Hudson estuary as prime habitat.

In August 1985 federal judge Thomas Griesa, while rejecting all air pollution arguments, also ruled that in their assessments and testimony the Federal Highway Administration and the US Army Corps of Engineers had failed to comply with the Clean Water Act and the National Environmental Policy Act. When an appeal of that ruling failed, the city caved. Westway was suddenly dead, a "triumph of People Power over the Establishment," as Phillip Lopate termed it in his book *Waterfront*.

Surprising as that outcome was, what happened in its aftermath, over the next quarter century, was no less so. In 1987 a task force appointed by the city and state recommended that the replacement for the West Side Highway consist of a six-lane urban boulevard, far less expensive than the Westway tunnel, to be built not below but at grade and flanked along the shoreline by clusters of facilities that would encourage human contact with the waterfront. A West Side Waterfront Panel, composed of people representing a broad range of interests, was convened in 1988. Its report proposed design guidelines for the roadway, an adjacent esplanade, and the restoration and public use of thirteen public piers between Battery Park City and Fifty-Ninth Street. The panel produced a "Vision Statement for the Hudson River Waterfront Park" that recommended creating the Hudson River Park Conservancy to plan, build, and help fund the park.

In 1995, with help from design consultants Quennell Rothschild Associates/Signe Nielsen, the conservancy issued a Concept and Financial Plan for the park that, according to one summary document, emphasized "the river as a great natural and recreational resource; the cultural and human history of the river and its waterfront; and connections to Manhattan's west-side neighbors." Facilities for nonmotorized boating were prominently proposed, as were lookouts, "get-downs" making direct access to the water easier, and creation or preservation of habitats for fish, birds, and native plants.

Local community boards, and landscape architects they selected to work on segments of the route, had been influential in shaping this grand design, with the help of countless charrettes and community gatherings. The Concept and Financial Plan emerging from these sessions oozed enthusiasm: "This park, within the next ten years, can heal an old wound, reclaim a long-forgotten heritage, and give birth to a glorious new one.... It will feature an array of active and passive recreation uses. The entire area will be graced by a waterside esplanade as well as a continuous, tree-lined bicycle path.... It's a place where parents and teachers can help educate their children about the ecology and history of the Hudson. It's a place for enjoying art and watching the boats sail by. And it's also a place for running, playing, sitting and sunning."

Trade-in funds from the interstate highway account would pep up the city's subway system, which at the time was badly run down. Suspicions lurked, though, with activist opponents of Westway resurfacing, voicing apprehensions about construction delays and the threat of over-commercialism. A community-based Alliance to Save Hudson River Park was formed in 1996 and claimed victory when in 1998 New York State governor George Pataki signed a law creating the Hudson River Park Trust to continue planning, building, and managing the property. In 1999 the alliance became a new private nonprofit, titled Friends of Hudson River Park, with watchdog and fund-raising responsibilities.

Long-delayed construction ensued, with the Friends effectively agitating for action, and progressed steadily over the 2000s. As of fall 2011, the park was 80 percent built, with work continuing at several key sites but with final completion likely to take another five years or more, thanks to the scarcity of public funds. As finally designed, the park encompasses some 150 upland acres featuring a five-mile ribbon of bicycle paths and walkways, as well as the thirteen recreational finger piers extending out into the river that were designated as "dedicated exclusively to park use." An additional 400 water acres constitute an estuarine reserve.

Specifically not allowed within the park are residential or commercial office or warehousing structures, hotels, casino or riverboat gambling, most motorized aircraft, amusement parks, television or film studios, commercial cinemas, and parking lots. The law specified that the park would offer recreational, entertainment, and education opportunities, that its design would recognize the importance of protecting wildlife habitat while offering economic benefits as well.

Today the Hudson River Park welcomes a remarkable seventeen million visitors a year. As many as eleven million of them use the park itself. The rest are headed for other independent attractions within the park's boundaries, such as the sightseeing fleet, the retired aircraft carrier *Intrepid* (on whose flight deck, as a naval aviator, I had landed my trainer plane in 1957), and the commercially operated Chelsea Piers sports complex. The park is no mere highway. The passing traffic notwithstanding, it has also become a giant playpen for space-squeezed New Yorkers badly in need of a new one. Lopate called it an "outdoor temple of physical culture."

"Once a dilapidated remnant of New York's industrial past," wrote Hudson River Park Trust chair Diana Taylor in the trust's annual message for 2011, "the Hudson River waterfront is now a blue and green playground for the whole city to enjoy."

And what of Route 9A, the roadway that had temporarily replaced the West Side Highway? "Instead of tunneling through landfill," reported the *Times*, "a six-to-eight lane street-level boulevard was built with computer-controlled signals." The New York State Department of

Transportation team working on the details were "true believers," says the Hudson River Park Trust's Noreen Doyle, as the design for the park was slowly worked out. "They worked hard to plan it the right way." Major entrances to the park were incorporated into every crosswalk and thought through with loving care within an agency widely known for insensitivity. They claim that vehicular traffic is moving relatively well along this corridor.

I tested this hypothesis by taking a weekday drive southward from the George Washington Bridge to the Holland Tunnel in Lower Manhattan during weekday business hours. Though pinned to the curb lane by a double-decker sightseeing bus and a CVS tractor-trailer, I was stopped by red traffic lights only twice—once at Forty-Second Street and again at Fourteenth.

On a brisk, windy Sunday morning, I set off by rented bicycle to ride the whole ten-mile circuit, starting from Pier 84 at the foot of Forty-Fourth Street in Midtown. Along here the park is squeezed in between commercial enterprises. There are piers for the Circle Line excursion boats and a successful water taxi company. Just north lies the *Intrepid*, her decks laden with aircraft, including a stray Concorde. North of that is an array of piers once used by classic ocean liners, now consigned to cruise ships, of which five were in port when I pedaled by.

But as I continued northward, away from these timeworn spots, I soon found myself in engaging new shoreline spaces at the northern end of the Hudson River Park and an adjoining southern extension of Riverside Park, a widely admired Robert Moses creation in the 1930s. Large numbers of bikers and skateboarders crowded the narrow bikeway. Along the esplanade between the bikeway and the water were handsomely landscaped areas attracting dog walkers and parents with babies in strollers. A part of town that had long remained an abandoned clutter of unused railroad lines was now dominated by a massive

Donald Trump housing development. In its shadow I dismounted, sat on a bench, and watched monarch butterflies en route to their winter habitats in Mexico. At Pier 84, a magnet for residents of the adjacent Hell's Kitchen neighborhood, there is a well-used launching float for kayakers and other small-boaters. Near the *Intrepid* I watched a solo fisherman casting lures from his spinning reel into the murky waters.

Farther south, past Pier 76, where the city underuses valuable shoreline space to park impounded cars, a small heliport at Thirtieth Street, from which sightseeing flights are now banned, still serves commercial customers. But south of here the Hudson River Park really kicks in. From the Chelsea community in the West Twenties to the Financial District at Battery Park City, recreation-minded visitors face a dazzling array of choices. There are handsome allocations of carefully landscaped gardens, granite paving, and grassy enclaves for sunbathing and picnicking, many playgrounds, and a carousel. Signs along the bikeway implore you to take advantage of the park's facilities: Swim, Sail, Fish, Blade, Board. Relax. Enjoy. Ride.

I saw helmetless teenage skateboarders testing fate at several challenging skate parks, tennis players, beach volleyball courts open for business, miniature golf being played. Sadly, I also saw a girl sitting on the pavement, her head heavily bandaged after a bicycling crash. At three Chelsea Piers, many kinds of sports including ice hockey were being played. Hundreds of golfers inside a huge cage were hitting balls out toward the river. A wide assortment of pleasure craft, including the Forbes family's "capitalist tool," the lavish *Highlander*, were berthed there.

From Chelsea down to the southern end of the park, a succession of handsomely landscaped gardens welcomed me. Trees and plants carefully selected to attract birds and butterflies line the bikeway and the adjacent pedestrian walkway. A particular standout is the garden area at Chelsea Cove on Piers 62 and 63. Here quite newly installed is a luscious garden, fashioned by a team that included the well-known landscape designer Lynden Miller, which forms a link between the city and the water. On this ground Miller, who according to the *Wall Street Journal* "creates urban Edens," has assembled an exuberant space with a profusion of trees, grasses, and blooming plantings of a wide variety of perennials within raised, gracefully curving beds. Hydrangeas and dahlias are featured. Chairs and tables under large patio umbrellas were well occupied when I dismounted and strolled past this highly appealing "entry garden" onto 9.5 acres of mostly open waterside parkland.

Beyond the piers, many small-boat sailors and kayakers were bobbing about despite the stiff breeze and choppy waters. In cities elsewhere in the United States, urban sailing is a well-established and widely shared custom. Office workers along Chicago's Michigan Boulevard have long been accustomed to slipping away for quick late afternoon sails in the shadow of the skyscrapers. The same goes for Bostonians and the Charles River. San Francisco Bay, for all its strong currents, heavy winds, and chilly fog banks, is seldom without plenty of sailboat traffic for most of the year.

But for all the appeal of the Statue of Liberty and the dramatic panorama of Lower Manhattan as seen from the water, few have until recently seen the Hudson as a place to go for a sail—or thought much about sailing as a recreational or educational activity. But, wrote Stacey Szewczyk in *Sailing* magazine, new trends including "the development of the city's waterfront as public green space have since widened New Yorkers' perceptions of its recreational potential."

Journeyman sailor Bill Bahen saw an opportunity to introduce New York City teenagers to the Hudson, unfamiliar to them despite its proximity, and to sailing. His sprightly nonprofit organization on Pier 40 in Chelsea, called Hudson River Community Sailing (HRCS), teaches them sailing skills aboard a fleet of eight donated twenty-four-foot sloops and runs a winter boat-building workshop. A thriving membership and charter program for adults has grown rapidly since it was launched in 2008. Several other similar organizations now serve this trade, giving more and more New York straphangers new glimpses of what for many of them is an entirely new watery world. "Get a taste of sailing," Bahen's group advises, adding that its two-hour crewed sails (eighty dollars per person) are "the perfect way to escape NYC without actually leaving."

The park caters to the mind as well as the body. Offerings range from concerts to film screenings, environmental education programs for adults and children, and a periodic Pier 84 event called Moon-Dance that attracts up to three thousand people on a pleasant evening. Some complain that the park pays insufficient attention to the Hudson shoreline's rich steamship culture and maritime history. A notable rejoinder is its friendly partnership with the nonprofit organization Save Our Ships New York, which operates the retired 130-foot fire-boat *John J. Harvey* out of her home base at Pier 66, an old Lackawanna Railroad property. This sturdy vessel, built in 1931, remained in active and distinguished service for New York City's fire department for sixty-three years, helping fight the world-famous fire aboard the French luxury liner *Normandie* in 1942.

Her finest hour came at the World Trade Center on 9/11. "There were a few people aboard that morning," says *Harvey* volunteer Renee Stanley, "and they saw it all happen. They realized that they were needed, and even though they lacked a full crew they went on down the river and stayed on station for 80 hours. They rescued 150 people who had no other way out." Stanley is one among many volunteers who help maintain and operate the old boat, conducting visitor tours, offering educational opportunities for school groups, and traveling the region's waterways to teach people elsewhere about marine history and water-front revitalization. From time to time they also crank up the boat's ultrapowerful Courtenay pumps to "squirt some water." The boat is now listed among "America's Treasures" on the National Register of Historic Places and seems destined to enjoy a long life.

As I continued my ride down to the park's southern end at Battery Park City in the Financial District, I pondered the plusses and minuses, with opinions still sharply split on who won and who lost what in the great effort to reconnect Lower Manhattan with its Hudson shorefront. Westway planner Craig Whitaker, an enthusiast who gave community groups some seven hundred presentations on the project, continues to think that the outcome was "a tragedy, a sad one," and "a missed oppor-tunity to create a vast amount of parkland at federal expense," reported *Downtown Express.* "Whitaker thinks Westway would have had a more accessible parkland than . . . some restored piers and the pierhead lines and some extremely narrow stretches with little more than a walkway and a bike path."

Phillip Lopate writes that the Westway advocates were much mis-understood and that their establishment, not the people, "had the pro-gressive vision and imagination." Architect Jaquelin Robertson, whose planning and design firm Cooper, Robertson & Partners has collabo-rated with architect Renzo Piano and the Whitney Museum to plan and design its new downtown premises at the foot of the High Line, is an outspoken Moses admirer. "He was one of the most brilliant public works planners in the history of the world," says Robertson. "Westway was a bold, Moses-like idea—take a big road and hide it underneath the water."

In contrast, he dismisses the Hudson River Park as an exercise in "patchwork creativity," consistent with New York City's still being a "Dutch trading town where it's always about money first." Clean Air

Action's Marcy Benstock unwaveringly feels that the Hudson River Park Trust and the Route 9A planners constitute stalking horses behind which lurk real estate interests ready to pounce as soon as possible. She complained to the *Times* that the park has taken too long to build, is a breeder of congestion from commercial ventures, and is "insufficiently accountable to the public." Lopate trashes the Hudson River Park as "an uninspiring compromise—a landscaped transit corridor that calls itself a park." Some community activists complain not only about the park's design but also about a corporate-style management culture at the trust that contrasts sharply with freer-wheeling but powerful forces at work within the shorefront communities. Too often, critics contend, buttoned-down trust executives favor tidy projects over those that reflect the neighborhood's boisterous seafaring past.

Those who admire the Hudson River Park continue to think that Westway planner Sam Ratensky and his associates represented what influential *Village Voice* columnist Mary Perot Nichols called the "dead hand of the past." Lawyer Al Butzel, speaking for a wide range of park enthusiasts, insists that Westway was still "ultimately a real estate and transportation plan with a few amenities." Its car-centric planners, he insists, would never have strayed as far afield, incorporating the needs of sailors and paddlers, let alone striped bass, as has the broad vision that has guided the Hudson River Park. The culture of the Westway option, he concludes, would have been "far less lively than what we have out there now."

"Just look at it," says the Hudson River Park Trust's board chair Diana Taylor. "I can't believe anybody could be against this. But they're still out there."

At the end of the day, I reckon, Manhattan would have won either way. Pressures from community advocates influenced the Hudson River Park's design. So would they have done much to soften Westway's hard edges and ward off insensitive developer initiatives. Both plans would address traffic-flow requirements. Both would transform an isolated and decadent edge of Manhattan into a vibrant set of thriving communities—Clinton, Chelsea, Tribeca—to the great benefit of residents and visitors. And the links between the park and the Hudson represent only the beginning of that transformation, with a new array of art galleries, cafes, restaurants, and stores replacing the seedy bars and strip joints that had long adorned that part of town. From Midtown all the way south to Battery Park City, as seen from the upper deck of a water taxi, an array of new office and residential buildings has created a handsome new stretch of skyline and greatly boosted real estate values in that part of the city.

Moreover, the Whitney Museum's 2008 decision to vacate its Upper East Side premises and build a far larger space on Gansevoort and Washington Streets, at the southern end of the High Line, gives the meatpacking district another mighty step forward toward cultural distinction. By the mid-2000s the museum, a prime showcase for twentieth-century and contemporary art, with an important collection of more than nineteen thousand objects and a lively schedule of events and education activities, was badly in need of more space. Its building on chic Madison Avenue, built in 1966 to a distinctive design by Marcel Breuer, had served the museum well. But more space had become a pressing need, and in its search for real estate, the museum had acquired several small buildings in its neighborhood. But, says architect Scott Newman of the Cooper, Robertson firm, "Out of that space they couldn't get the museum they really wanted. They do a lot of work with living artists; they need really big open galleries. So in 2006 they had the courage to abandon that effort and look elsewhere."

There were multiple sites, generally downtown, big enough to accommodate a large footprint but not too tall, usually with an industrial history. Out of this search there emerged a productive working partnership between New York City, the meatpackers remaining in the neighborhood, and the Whitney that resulted in the museum's purchase of the new site on Gansevoort Street, adjacent to the southern entrance to the High Line and just a few steps away from the Hudson River park. Groundbreaking for the airy two-hundred-thousand-square-foot structure, with fifty thousand square feet of interior gallery space, took place in 2011, with the building's public opening expected in 2015.

In many respects the project reflects a spirit of cooperation between the institution and the community. In advance of setting a design, the Whitney took the initiative by meeting repeatedly with community groups, especially the Greenwich Village Society of Historic Preservation. Concerns expressed included traffic and noise, especially at night, and fears that the Whitney would push out meatpackers still in the area. Satisfied with regard to these typical issues, community leaders could then appreciate the positive values the Whitney would bring: an eighty-five-hundred-square-foot cantilevered terrace along Gansevoort Street that would serve as a sheltered public gathering place; a big open space connecting the High Line to the Hudson River Park; large windows facing west, allowing visitors to look from the building at the park and the river; shopping and eating facilities that would attract other such businesses. Already, says Scott Newman, "everybody who lives in the neighborhood values the Whitney as a real anchor in an evolving community. It's a natural fit."

It took major forces in New York's City Hall and in the private sector to bring about and fund the High Line and the Hudson River Park. It is therefore encouraging to note the flowering of a bustling new Hudson economy along the city's shoreline under those big protective umbrellas. In 2011 evidence came in the form of reactions to a wastewater discharge into the river resulting from a fire that caused the closure of a sewage treatment plant in Harlem. "Sewage Discharge Sidelines Businesses," reported the *New York Times*, which cited "devastating" consequences for swim clubs, kayak rental and sailboat charter companies, and operators of children's summer camps after the city "prohibited or strongly discouraged" recreation on the river at the midsummer height of the business season.

"This may not be a lot for Goldman Sachs," said one Hudson frontiersman, operator of a kayak company that had lost as much as ten thousand dollars in business, "but it could not have been a more direct shot into the heart of our season." Shorefront businesses hardly welcomed that kind of attention. But that there should even be such a season shows the depth of the changes along the city's Hudson shoreline, described in the *Times* as a place where a new breed of entrepreneurs has arrived, "determined to transform the filthy industrial waterway slicked with oily rainbows into an aquatic playground fit for a 21st-century city."

CHAPTER 11

Albany Stew

A FREQUENT COMPLAINT RAISED BY HUDSON VALLEY LEADERS IS THAT New York, as a home rule state, gives officials and planning boards in small communities free rein to make local land-use decisions without reference to regional needs or opportunities or coordination of any sort on planning, zoning, or land use. The result, said *Hudson Valley* magazine, is "a patchwork of inconsistent zoning requirements across the region." The magazine invited comment from two prominent Hudsonians representing sharply different sectors but in some respects agreeing on what is needed.

The problem, said Scenic Hudson's Ned Sullivan, is "the lack of a shared vision as to what constitutes good development. We need a shared recognition to preserve what makes the Valley so unique and beautiful." Real estate magnate Martin Ginsburg, who has underway a major project on yet another abandoned waterfront site in the town of Haverstraw, agreed that "Long term vision is solely (*sic*) lacking throughout the Hudson River Valley. It's pathetic how such a major resource is totally neglected. Everything is done piecemeal."

In 2009, when the valley celebrated the four-hundredth anniversary of Henry Hudson's epic cruise upriver aboard the *Half Moon*, Joan Davidson of the Hudson town of Germantown, a veteran of many high positions in the public and private sectors, saw an opportunity to generate a broad new vision for the future. Appointed chair of the Hudson-Fulton-Champlain Quadricentennial Commission, with a mandate to reach beyond the hoopla, giving the celebration a theme or direction that would justify a substantial extra investment of state funds, the arrestingly handsome, silver-haired Davidson resolved to seize the high ground and use the "Quad" as a showcase to prepare and display a "vision and practical agenda" for the valley.

Numerous actions, extending well beyond the "eco-docks" initiative mentioned earlier, were taken to advance the ambitious "Quad" agenda. Listening sessions were held in six communities. An interactive website called Ourhudson.org was established, giving anyone a chance to participate in the visioning. Six working groups composed of distinguished leaders, each to survey a sector of Hudson life and agree on recommendations for future public initiatives, were constituted. What became apparent during the Quad ceremonies, states OurHudson's welcome page, was that "there is a real opportunity now to bring focus to the Hudson River Valley's long spoken-of but yet to be fully-realized potential. . . . The river needs a practical agenda, not platitudes. . . . A real Agenda for the Hudson with goals and milestones will be a good guide for elected leaders now in office and candidates aspiring to replace them."

Disappointingly few citizens took advantage of the chance to participate via submissions to the website's public comments section. Others grumbled. "We need more money, not more plans," said one seasoned veteran of too many easel-boarded, facilitated "visioning" exercises. But the task forces delivered an interesting and challenging, if not always new, set of ideas.

The Culture & Education group reminded viewers that the valley was the center of the American Revolution, the Industrial Revolution, and the Environmental Preservation Revolution. Echoing the thoughts of Dr. Partridge a century ago and Congressman Maurice Hinchey in more recent times, the panel proposed that the valley be redefined as "a national park that positions the region as a nationally significant cultural, historical, and environmental center." Within the park, the Environmental Science Center of America would "showcase the biodiversity, ecosystem health, and environmental attributes of our region" through public programs, exhibitions, and educational work.

The Economic Development team saw opportunities for more aggressive branding and marketing of valley products in New York City, better creation and promotion of tourism incentives, the establishment of "waterfront development zones" to build on initial reconnecting with the river successes such as that of Beacon, and partnerships with high-technology learning centers that would grow the region's knowledge economy and enable young Hudsonians to stay home and remain competitive. It saw the future Hudson Valley as "a region where towns and cities are open for business twenty-four hours a day to create more vibrant, multi-dimensional local economies." Enactment of supporting mechanisms, said the group, "will require local policy leaders to overcome political hurdles and the dysfunctional policy making process in Albany."

As for ways to keep farmers farming in the valley, Judy LaBelle's agriculture group stressed state support for "the development of new agricultural products that allow farmers to diversify and enhance their economic vitality" and advanced a series of promotional ideas including, interestingly, "an integrated approach to tourism and agriculture, like that of the Po Valley in Italy." LaBelle tidily capsuled her dream:

The Hudson Valley is universally recognized as a world class landscape producing world class food. The Hudson Valley and the Napa Valley are coastal brackets for a country that has

187

rediscovered its respects for food and for the people, water, and land that produce it. The importance of agriculture to the region's quality of life—its economic and environmental well-being and the health of its residents—is understood and supported by public officials at every level . . . The Valley stands as a national model for how the many and complex components of a major metropolitan region can work together to support a food and agricultural system that benefits all residents.

The Land Use, Energy, and Environment team issued myriad recommendations, emphasizing the need for development without sprawl, waterfront revitalization, protection of undeveloped land resources, empowerment for the Hudson River Greenway, greater attention to brownfield cleanups, and the transformation of the valley into "a model and showcase for clean, safe, and renewable energy." Among the committee's proposals were measures that would directly affect slum dwellers' quests for a better life, calling for "strong incentives for infill development" and "a streamlined permitting process and state programs that invest in downtowns."

The Transportation panel stressed the need for "new incentives to reduce truck traffic and better utilize existing freight networks while exploring the use of waterborne freight options where economically feasible to avoid further highway congestion and make it easier for farmers to get their goods to market." The overdue replacement of the antique trans-Hudson Tappan Zee Bridge is also flagged as an urgent, if high-priced need.

Putting these and many other ideas together, Congressman Maurice Hinchey told the Open Space Institute that he sees a "great opportunity" for the Hudson over the current century, especially because of its "huge, wonderful" history as a valuable resource for the nation. The

New York League of Conservation Voters likewise has an exhaustive policy agenda, calling for actions that "cost little or nothing yet will generate important economic activity." The league favors an emphasis on clean, renewable energy technologies, especially solar. As regards statewide planning for sustainable development, the league wants smart-growth initiatives to be rewarded by means of competitive grant making. It wants better protection for farmland and greater efficiency for the state's transportation network. It wants more money to protect the state's environment and maintain and preserve open space, calling for increases in polluter and user fees and for Environmental Protection Fund support to reach 2 percent of the state's budget by 2015. Especially highlighted in the league's 2011 Policy Agenda is the caveat that "If the state moves forward with hydraulic fracturing [in the Marcellus Shale] it must have regulations in place to protect the state's natural resources and human health."

In September 2011 the OurHudson group literally floated their ideas, taking them aboard Pennsylvania Railroad Barge No. 399 for a multicity tour of the shoreline from Hudson to Yonkers. This innovative barnstorming program was seen as the Quad project's last hurrah—a final crash attempt to bring the ideas and constituency it had developed, and was still creating, into play for the longer term. The sturdy steel-hulled covered barge, built in 1943 and used for many years to ship coffee and other commodities upstream from the Hudson's mouth, now carried promotional materials from OurHudson, Scenic Hudson, the Department of Environmental Conservation, Riverkeeper, and other concerned groups. Also loaded aboard was projection equipment to show clips from an unfinished twenty-eight-minute film, *Hudson Rising*, commissioned by OurHudson to highlight the promise of shoreline revitalization activities. Stopovers and events were planned from mid-September to well into October, with a grand finale in Hudson.

I caught up with Pennsy 399 while she was tied up at Rondout Landing near the Hudson River Maritime Museum at the heart of Kingston's waterfront. It was a pleasantly cool September Saturday, and the scene reflected both this shoreline's high potential and the difficulties of getting there. Abandoned lots and buildings attested to the downfall of Kingston as a hub for the transport to New York City of bluestone, bricks, coal, and other heavy freight. Long-unused tugboats and World War II–vintage PT boats lay around awaiting restoration. Several sailing vessels, including the handsome old schooner *Lettie G. Howard,* showed few signs of recent use. Boarded-up houses lined some of the side streets.

Yet also, on murky water painted a deep reddish-brown by flooding from the recent Hurricane Irene, paddlers aboard a brave little fleet of kayaks stroked vigorously upstream. An eight-oared shell was out practicing. A couple in a canoe was fishing, casting a lure from a spinning rod. Boat owners were tinkering at the marinas. A couple of blocks inland, at a natural amphitheater called Cornell Park, a lively "free outdoor drum celebration" called Drum Boogie was fully underway, with several groups working out intricate Steve Reich rhythms before a rapt audience.

"Great park, great city," enthused Ulster County executive Mike Hein, adding that "we have more artists per capita than any other place in the US. That's what makes this such a special place." Restaurants were doing good business: by the time I got to a deli, the proprietor had run out of many staples.

At the courtyard adjacent to the maritime museum, board members and other dignitaries and the usual suspects were gathering for its annual fund-raiser. Aboard the barge filmmaker Jasper Goldman showed clips of his *Hudson Rising* to a rapt audience. There were many speeches and much discussion about the museum's new alliance with the Clearwater organization, which involves homeporting the famous sloop at the museum's landing and building a new education center incorporating a boat-building workshop. Reads a brochure jointly published by the two organizations: "Clearwater builds strong boats with kids, Hudson River Maritime Museum builds strong kids with boats; together we build a stronger community."

OurHudson won its share of praise and awards. The scene buzzed with talk of new projects and ideas, including plans for Kingston's renaissance as a working waterfront as well as a recreational and educational center. Said Jeff Rumpf, Clearwater's energetic executive director: "This is an area with a real edge to it. There are many examples of opportunities slipping away with the bad economy. But there are also amazing things happening."

What help do groups and ideas of these sorts get from the state government in Albany? Precious little, according to a watchdog outfit called Environmental Advocates of New York that delivers frequent rants against red tape, using conservation-earmarked state funds for general purposes, and gross inefficiency. In Albany, with occasional exceptions, the conservationist passions of both Roosevelt governorships then subsided with periodic expressions of good intentions but often inadequate follow-through and budget shortfalls.

In view of these and many other complaints, it would be difficult to award Albany an "A" for recent decades of environmental policy affecting the Hudson Valley. But a "B" seems in order, with a special plaudit for Governor Mario Cuomo (1983–94), a gold star for three-term (1995–2006) governor George Pataki, and a provisional accolade for Andrew Cuomo (Mario's son), who was off to a solid start after his first year in office in economically troubled 2011.

Dig-we-must policies prevailed under Governor Nelson Rockefeller (1959–73), whose two billion dollar, Soviet-style Empire State

Plaza in Albany stands as a classically inappropriate, taxpayer-financed model for a gentle rural landscape rich in apple orchards and farmland. *Battlestar Galactica* on the Hudson, one of many severe critics called it. Platoons of high towers claw skyward from bare ground, the principal one reaching fully forty-four stories in height. Lower skyscrapers march along a mall stretching southward from the original Beaux Arts state capitol building. A whole neighborhood was flattened to make way for these buildings, with expressways to match, and what had been a congenial town was permanently disfigured. The new highway system, writes David Stradling in his book *The Nature of New York*, made it easy for drivers to move between nearby interstate highways and downtown parking garages, "but it also separated the entire city from the Hudson River, and it filled valuable urban acres with tangles of interchanges."

The project, launched in 1959 and not completed until 1976, set a pattern of mediocrity in land-use planning for the Capital Region and beyond, or in many instances no planning at all. Principal features listed by the Open Space Institute in a 2005 study: rapid growth in population and residential development, soaring property taxes, major losses in farmland and wetlands, and the usual characteristics of dominant sprawl. OSI's report cried out for efforts to control sprawl "on a broad framework with a regional perspective" and use home rule not as a means of tolerating mediocrity but as an "opportunity" for communities to "adopt the principles that will allow our region to grow, yet continue to be an area of productive farms, historical landscapes, quiet hidden places, and open spaces." Cities as far away as Poughkeepsie, fifty miles south of Albany, where a complex new highway system killed the center of town for decades until the Walkway Over the Hudson finally came to the rescue, also fell victim to what Stradling called "the anti-urban thinking that dominated modernist architecture."

Of course there is more to Nelson Rockefeller's conservation legacy than Empire State Plaza. Had the state not anted up the full $500,000 that the Church family was asking for Olana, a developer would most likely have gotten control of that priceless land and, in the absence of any zoning at the time, permanently disfigured it. Rockefeller joined others in his family in planning the partial opening up of their Pocantico Hills property and the establishment of Historic Hudson Valley and other new institutions in the Tarrytown/Sleepy Hollow region that are much enjoyed by neighbors and tourists alike. Influenced by the aggressive style of the headstrong master builder Robert Moses, who favored the idea of a large and unified state park system, Rockefeller sponsored two successful bond bills providing $125 million for the acquisition of lands for recreation. But for all that, the heavy-handedness of Nelson Rockefeller's style, when it came to Con Edison's Storm King proposal or the expressway that he wanted to build on the Hudson's east bank, marks him as a generally negative influence on the Hudson Valley environment.

Under the succeeding regimes of governors Malcolm Wilson and Hugh Carey, little was done to improve the record. But then there came a succession of wise public-sector environmental initiatives that also encouraged or brought about land preservation and protection—especially during the governorships of Democrat Mario Cuomo and Republican George Pataki. In many respects in recent years, until the demise of Governor Eliot Spitzer and the miserable performance of his successor, David Paterson, state actions have tended to reinforce the general swing back from mid-twentieth-century apathy and neglect to mindful planning and greater concern for the region's environment.

Though Mario Cuomo was a downstate-oriented governor and showed limited interest in environmental matters, he did try for a major environmental bond issue in 1990 (it failed at the ballot box thanks to pressures from upstate opponents) and worked effectively with New York City officials on watershed protection issues. The innovative piece of legislation called the Hudson River Valley Greenways Act of 1991 was brought to Cuomo by Laurance Rockefeller and environmental lawyer Henry Diamond, his longtime associate on environmental and conservation matters. Diamond had spent many years of service in New York State, including a tour of duty as the state's first environmental commissioner starting in 1970. The problem he saw was that rational regional planning for open space preservation and efficient land use was inhibited by the sheer number of competing small jurisdictions in the valley, all putting forward planning and zoning ordinances without coordinating with neighbors and all, says Diamond, "racing for the tax base."

The Greenway law that Rockefeller and Diamond proposed would remain consistent with the state's tradition of home rule while also creating "a process for voluntary regional cooperation among 264 communities within 13 counties that border the Hudson River." Under the law, as signed in 1991 by a sympathetic if not enthusiastic Mario Cuomo, a "Greenway Council" would work with local counties and municipalities toward the development of "a voluntary regional planning compact" for the entire valley. Small local decisions would be studied for their regional impact. The Greenway Conservancy, a "public benefit corporation" with grant-making capabilities, "coordinates efforts to establish a Hudson River Valley trail system, promote the Hudson River Valley as a single tourism destination area, assist in the preservation of agriculture and strengthen state agency cooperation with local governments." Greenway principles highlight green features such as walkable, mixed use urban centers, saving farmland, and retrofitting old commercial strips.

The program uses its own very limited grant-making capabilities to encourage municipalities to do more. Initial planning activities in Dutchess County, for example, prompted the county itself to chip in almost ten million dollars in matching funds for open space and farmland protection.

A particularly attentive Greenways customer has been the Northern Dutchess Alliance, which brings together nine towns and villages north and east of Poughkeepsie (including Rhinebeck, the fashionable spot where Chelsea Clinton was married); many around there can afford to take the time to do Greenways chores. Businesses and environmental organizations chip in. "Early on they had the political will to do a Greenway Compact," said planner Mark Castiglione, who in 2011 was doubling as acting director of the Greenways program and of the Hudson River Valley National Heritage Area. "They had bipartisan buy-in and a wealth of talented volunteers. In that area there's always a new Greenway project going on." One recent one: a buy-local campaign.

According to Castiglione, Greenways "strikes a balance between regional coordination and the traditional home rule powers that New York State communities enjoy."

"The Greenway has all the right ingredients," says Ned Sullivan. "It's bottom up, it establishes partnerships between local communities, it has defused initial fears about property rights." The program has been quietly gaining strength in recent years, with swarms of enthusiastic volunteers faithfully signing petitions and attending meetings, and achieving buy-in from 90 percent of the communities within its area. In recent times of budget gloom, the hard-pressed program was struggling for survival. But successes were still being claimed, and future activities planned.

I asked Henry Diamond if the program had lived up to his expectations. "I really don't know," said Diamond. "I haven't lived in New York for many years. But the program is still around after twenty years. That says something."

Pataki grew up in the Hudson Valley, had a farming background, was sensitive to landscape issues, and wins widespread acclaim for his environmental performance. As a private citizen he had chaired Westchester County's land trust. He birds. In Albany he championed annual appropriations for the state's Environmental Protection Fund, which in combination with revenues from a successful $1.75 billion Clean Water/Clean Air bond act passed in 1995, resulted in the state's protecting over a million acres of open space, over twelve years, by the end of his third term in 2006. The park system was expanded by 25 percent, and twenty-six new state parks were created.

These are statistics of which Pataki, says his former chief of staff John Cahill, is particularly proud. Pataki also nurtured innovative activities, such as the brightest days of the state's coastal resources management program, then a very creative planning agency working effectively with local communities in the Hudson estuary, as well as along Long Island Sound and the Atlantic shoreline. He gave quiet but important backing for those opposing St. Lawrence Cement in Hudson. "I'm very environmental," he told NRDC's John Adams during a chance railroad station meeting long ago, when he was first running for a seat in the state assembly. "I really care about those things." Pataki also played an important role in saving the splendid Adirondacks from checkerboard development, saw and promoted the links between environmental protection and economic advancement, and overall merits an accolade as the state's most environmentally committed governor ever and a national leader in the field among state-level politicians.

Another signal state accomplishment has been the creation and enlargement, thanks to a series of successful bond issues and occasional acts of bountiful private philanthropy, of its magnificent array of 178 parks and 35 historical sites encompassing 325,000 acres. The system had its origins in the 1880s, when vast tracts in the Adirondacks and a 33,000-acre section of the Catskills became a "Forest Preserve" and later the basis for the giant Adirondack Park, the initial motivation being not to preserve wilderness but to sequester land for future timber cutting. Later, with this park at the northern end of the state, and to the south the antiquarrying movement saving the Palisades and forming the basis of the Palisades Interstate Park (PIPC), the dots began to connect.

Bear Mountain State Park near West Point opened in 1913, attracted one million visitors the following year, and has been bustling ever since. The Palisades Interstate Parkway, a beautiful piece of highway architecture connecting to the splendid Bear Mountain and George Washington Bridges, opened in 1924 and in 1931 respectively. The magnificent new bridges cleared the way for hordes of New Yorkers to explore the Highlands and adjacent areas.

Not even the Great Depression did much to slow down the development of the system. During the 1930s John D. Rockefeller Jr. poured millions into the effort to strengthen the PIPC and keep out the quarrymen. Workers under President Roosevelt's popular Civilian Conservation Corps poured in to build infrastructure at Bear Mountain. With great help from environmental bond acts passed by the voters in 1972 and again in 1986, major land acquisitions were accomplished during those decades. Between 1996 and 2008, the system expanded by an additional 25 percent. Twenty-six new state parks came into being.

With some fifty-five million annual visitors in recent years, contributing major amounts to local economies and offering recreation and relief for city dwellers in a densely populated area, the system never looked like a good candidate for bureaucratic tampering. Yet capital budgets have been inadequate to prevent deterioration of basic needs such as sewage treatment and drinking water. Operating budgets have repeatedly been slashed, with grievous consequences for services. In the spring of 2010, Governor David Paterson took the unprecedented step of fully closing eighty-eight parks, amounting to 40 percent of the system, and planned to keep them closed during the busy summer season. Never before in 125 years, said the Open Space Institute, had the state closed its parks, despite the stresses of two world wars, the Great Depression, and numerous recessions.

Both houses of the state legislature reacted hotly. On the eve of Memorial Day weekend that year, just enough new money was found to rescue the rickety system. But the future still looked so precarious that the nonprofit Alliance for New York State Parks, with a mission to help protect their future and seek support from the private sector, was founded under the auspices of the Open Space Institute. Its chairperson is the highly respected Carol Ash, former administrator of the state's Office of Parks, Recreation, and Historic Preservation.

Another agency with a long view is the Hudson River Estuary Program, founded in 1987 as a coordinating mechanism that "engages stakeholders and advances science to keep the Hudson River clean and vibrant and the Hudson Valley green and prosperous." A division of the state's Department of Environmental Conservation, the Estuary Program commendably reaches out to nonprofits, including Clearwater and Riverkeeper, as well as to many other grassroots groups working within the Hudson between the river's mouth and the dam at Troy, where the tidal flow ends.

The Estuary Program also partners with scientific research organizations and federal agencies. It does much to inform often poorly informed local jurisdictions about addressing the needs of hard-pressed aquatic species as they plan for development. It maps. It educates. It gives small grants for community efforts. And it sets forth a clear agenda for actions to be taken over up to five years ahead. The program is brilliantly led by Frances Dunwell, also the author of two well received Hudson books. Yet this program too has been stifled for lack of funding, as its reports wistfully admit.

As for Washington, the valley has enjoyed occasional bursts of attention from federal legislators. One bright moment came in 1996 with the congressional designation of the valley as a National Heritage Area. Despite some confusion as to what such an area actually is and can do, this one has strengthened the links between historical sites in the valley, developed a stirring Master Plan for the future evolution of the program, put up a great website, and in other respects struggled to build itself a stronger network.

A tireless Hudson booster is Congressman Maurice Hinchey, who in 2011 began his tenth term representing an eight-county area, including several that border the river. Years ago he authored legislation leading to the National Heritage Area designation, and it helped him start thinking big about the valley's future. Along the way he has built what Hudson champion and Greenways chairman Barnabas McHenry calls an "incredible record of service to his constituents" on a wide range of issues, including wildlife, clean air and water, and solid waste. In 2010, with the wolf at the door, Hinchey was working hard to keep the state's parks open, warning Governor David Paterson that closing them would jeopardize funding for the state from the federal Land and Water Conservation Fund. He strongly favors tighter controls over fracking procedures planned by natural gas drillers for the Marcellus Shale.

In 2010, tearing yet another page out of Dr. Partridge's book from a century ago, Hinchey also maneuvered through the House the Hudson River Valley Special Resource Study Act, which would authorize the National Park Service (NPS) to "evaluate the national significance of the area" and the "suitability" of designating it as part of the National

Park System. Should NPS come up with a favorable recommendation, Hinchey pledged to introduce the necessary further legislation. The underlying idea remained constant: Achieving national park status for the region, even if the lands involved were scattered and not contiguous in the manner of a classic park, would release a much-needed new flow of federal dollars and resources for managing and improving parklands scattered throughout the region. The successful park system in the San Francisco Bay Area is a model. Done right, the federal designation could also give the valley an identity, a brand that would build the flow of tourists to the region.

The House passed Hinchey's bill in 2010, but it did not make it to the Senate floor. In 2011, despite the Republican takeover of the House, Hinchey reintroduced the bill and once again commenced the laborious process of steering it through the treacherous shallows of federal congressional action. At last report the bill was still slumbering in congressional committee, its future uncertain since Hinchey, after ten terms in office and a bout of colon cancer, decided not to run for re-election in 2012.

As for natural gas drilling, the federal Energy Policy Act of 2005 specifically excluded hydraulic fracturing from regulations provided by the Safe Drinking Water, Clean Air, and Clean Water Acts, leaving regulatory responsibility to affected states with differing priorities. This legislation also allows the drilling companies not to disclose the often highly toxic chemicals they add to the fracking liquid. A bill known as the FRAC (Fracturing Responsibility and Awareness of Chemicals) Act, which would delete the 2005 exemption and enable EPA to regulate fracking under the Safe Drinking Water Act, was introduced in both houses of Congress in June 2009. This effort never made it to the floor of either house and died with the 111th Congress that adjourned in January 2011.

Reintroduced in March 2011 in both houses, the FRAC Act remained once again bottled up in committee as of midyear, facing even stiffer opposition with the shift to Republican control of the House of Representatives. In the fall of 2010, Interior Secretary Ken Salazar angered some drillers by announcing his department's intention to develop new rules governing fracking on public lands. Warning of a citizen antifracking backlash, he talked of the need to disclose the chemicals used in the process. But as of mid-2011 he was maintaining a generally low profile on the whole subject.

In the fall of 2010, the League of Conservation Voters enthusiastically endorsed Mario Cuomo's son Andrew for governor, citing him as "the right choice for New York's environment" and as one who has "articulated a pragmatic, forward-thinking sustainability agenda that focuses on reviving New York's economy through smart growth and clean energy." Evidence of Cuomo's long-term commitment to the environment, the league continued, was to be found in his performance as Bill Clinton's secretary of the federal Department of Housing and Urban Development from 1997–2001 and later as New York State's attorney general.

In his 2010 campaign, despite severe budget constraints, Cuomo offered a comprehensive environmental agenda. "From the early stages of the conservation movement of the late 19th century to the environmental movement as we know it today," read an introductory passage of his 160-page "Cleaner, Greener NY" campaign document, "New York led the world on environmentalism. As Governor, Andrew Cuomo will ensure that we become a national environmental leader once again." Specifics about what exactly he would do to restore the state to that pinnacle were in relatively short supply, notwithstanding the document's impressive length, but it makes some key broad-picture points. Unlike his predecessors, Cuomo pledged to "ensure that the Environmental Protection Fund will be used for the purpose for which it was created." He pledged state support to restore blocked funds for farm-land protection, and "encourage the development and implementation of sustainable community planning" built around the central idea that "environmental protection is a critical economic driver."

Cuomo committed himself to further efforts to persuade the federal government not to renew the operating license of the earthquake- and tsunami-susceptible Indian Point nuclear power plant, only twenty-four miles north of the Bronx, when it comes up for review in 2013. The document also takes up what one state legislator called "the environmental issue of the century for New York state," speaking out stridently against any Marcellus Shale natural gas drilling "that might negatively affect any existing watershed." Watersheds are "sacrosanct," the document continues. "Andrew Cuomo would not support any drilling that would threaten the State's major sources of drinking water."

Early on, Cuomo made two nominations that delighted the state's environmental leaders. As commissioner of the state Office of Parks, Recreation, and Historic Preservation, he named Rose H. Harvey, a widely admired negotiator and communicator who worked for twenty-seven years at the Trust for Public Land (TPL). Said TPL's New York State director Leslie Wright: "Ms. Harvey's storied career in establishing parks, playgrounds and gardens in urban areas, combined with her ongoing advocacy for open space, makes her the ideal candidate to lead this agency."

As commissioner of the state Department of Environmental Conservation, Cuomo chose the equally well-regarded Joe Martens, president of the Open Space Institute since 1998 and previously deputy secretary for energy and the environment under former governor Mario Cuomo. With a budget-crunch-depleted staff and the huge Marcellus Shale drilling issue crowding his in-box and his calendar, Martens faces no lack of challenges. But he is widely thought to be equal to them, hailed as a deeply experienced conservationist and, as one peer put it, "a terrific fellow to deal with."

Of all the environmental concerns before Cuomo, the controversial business of natural gas drilling must rank as the most difficult. In states where fracking is a possibility and among many politicians as well as environmentalists, there is a growing sense of urgency. Pennsylvania, whose politicians are widely accused of being owned by Big Gas, has imposed limited public disclosure rules and, in response to a withering 2011 *New York Times* series about its management of the issue, instituted stiffened tax and regulatory measures. Pro-industry Wyoming, the source of 10 percent of all natural gas produced in the United States and scorned even by some ultraconservatives as the captive of the industry, surprisingly installed a public disclosure requirement, despite the industry's contention that the chemicals used are a valuable trade secret.

In the fall of 2010, New York legislators, as ever fearful of New York City watershed contamination, voted a moratorium on Marcellus fracking to give scientists a chance to learn more about its environmental effects. In December 2010 Paterson refused to sign their bill and vetoed it instead. Later, however, he issued his own decree calling for a moratorium on Marcellus drilling until July 2011. Cuomo called on Environmental Conservation Commissioner Martens to have his department complete its review on schedule, its agenda expanded to cover recent developments, and deliver a draft document for public comment by July 2011. Martens complied, tossing bones to both sides. The new draft rules, subject to subsequent refinement, would allow carefully managed drilling beneath 80 percent of the state's land but ban it entirely in the state's parklands, forests, and wildlife areas—and in the New York City and Syracuse watersheds. Controversially, the draft plan also allowed drilling as close as a thousand feet to New York City's fragile network of aqueducts and other water-supply infrastructure.

Not good enough, said NRDC's Kate Sinding. "There needs to be a buffer area in which there's no drilling whatsoever." Catskill Mountainkeeper Wes Gillingham saw the plan as a means of getting the camel's nose under the tent, en route to "creating a road map" for more intensive hydrofracking in New York. Martens, said to be personally opposed to fracking, argued that the proposed new rules are considerably tighter than those spelled out in a 2009 report. He irked some environmentalists by saying that they "strike the right balance between protecting our environment, watershed, and drinking water and promoting economic development."

Environmental leaders did agree, though, that the new analysis and recommendations represent a major improvement over the 2009 version. Waterkeeper Alliance president Robert F. Kennedy Jr., stating that Cuomo had assured him that "his goal is to have DEC put in place the most rigorous regulations in the 50 states governing shale gas extraction activities in New York," agreed to join Commissioner Martens's advisory panel. Turning down the invitation, he continued, would have been "counter-productive and chicken-hearted." Two NRDC staff members also signed on as advisers, with their organization noting "a boatload of unresolved issues and unanswered questions" to be addressed during the public comment period lasting at least until year-end. Serious flooding in the Catskills, in the wake of heavy rainfall from two tropical storms during the 2011 hurricane season, raised new concerns about fracking in floodplains and the disposal of toxic wastewater from fracking operations.

Above all, it was widely being argued, there was no incentive to rush. Many voices, including that of assembly Speaker Sheldon Silver, urged Cuomo to stay cool. "Governor Cuomo has the chance to get it right," said NRDC. "He must take all the time he needs to ensure fracking is not allowed to proceed until proven safe. The consequences of rushing ahead in New York—as we've seen around the country—are too grave to do otherwise."

Overall, as of late 2011 Cuomo was getting high marks even on environmental issues that were not his top priority. He had kept his campaign promise to maintain the Environmental Protection Fund intact at $134 million, the same level as in the previous fiscal year, which environmentalists considered a victory. He had so far refrained from following prior governors' frequent practice of raiding that cookie jar to cover shortfalls elsewhere. For the state's parks, he had come up with a lean budget but one sufficient to keep all but one or two of them up and running and avoiding a repeat of the prior year's confrontation over park closings. He had stood firmly behind his campaign pledge to shut down the aging Indian Point nuclear power plant even though experts were stressing the costs and complications that would accompany a closure. He had made first-class staff appointments. In an effort to stimulate regional approaches to economic development, he had appointed ten regional councils to offset the uncoordinated power wielded by "dozens of separate state and local agencies," as one handout put it.

And while working through the Marcellus Shale natural gas drilling details, he was doing his best to avoid polarization as the debate gathered strength during the fall of 2011 with the release of the state's keenly awaited fifteen-hundred-page Revised Draft Supplemental Generic Environmental Impact Statement (RDSGEIS), through which all concerned had begun poring with care. Environmentalists were continuing to insist that they needed extra time to examine what they see as a flawed document, claiming that Cuomo had sold out and that he and environmental commissioner Martens were fast-tracking the document and jeopardizing New York City's water supply. Martens countered, arguing that the state is not rushing and that its deliberations on the issue are "fair, intelligent, and open."

Not a bad record overall, considering Albany's fractious and often tumultuous political scene, and good enough to qualify as another reason to hope for progress on the ambitious OurHudson agenda.

CHAPTER 12

Resetting the Valley

IN DESCRIBING HOW CHANGING LIFESTYLES IN THE HUDSON VALLEY are playing into the hands of greater environmental protection and concern, I do not mean to argue that the valley has magically outpaced the nation in its quest for greatness. Not much less than many people elsewhere, the valley's residents remain attracted to conventional forms of consumption. I do believe, though, that high energy prices, stiff property taxes, the freedom and energy of cyberspace, a persistent shortage of traditional jobs, and the emergence of new values, are prompting more and more Hudsonians, particularly young adults, to make sharp and practical shifts in the way they want and can afford to live. For the most part these are economically beneficial shifts that also happen to nurture a cleaner environment. Eating healthier foods, for example.

A persuasive spokesman for these emerging new preferences is the urbanologist Richard Florida of the Rotman School of Management in Toronto. "We can literally feel the demise of the old suburban way of life all around us," Florida reports. He finds the US economy not writhing in the grip of the Great Recession but undergoing radical transformation for the better. His most recent book *The Great Reset* describes this shift away from dominant post–World War II aspirations—home ownership, suburban lifestyles, proliferating possessions—and toward a "new economic landscape" where industrial brawn is giving way to a surge of "knowledge, creativity, and ideas" that will "do for our times what suburbanization did for the postwar era." The new values will "ultimately power new kinds of demand and undergird a new round of economic growth," with creativity becoming "the single most important source of energy" to power the new economy.

In Florida's hierarchy, out are big Detroit cars, traffic congestion, subprime mortgage lenders, traditional patterns of consumption. In are Google, green products, rental housing, Zipcars, denser mixed-use communities replacing some of the outer residential suburbs. Members of Florida's new "creative class" want far more from the place they inhabit than what a seasonal second residence can provide. In the manner of his guru Jane Jacobs, Florida admires cozy urban neighborhoods where "eyes on the street" protect people who know each other. Parks, bike paths, cafes, walkable downtowns need to lie closer at hand, said Florida in his major work, *The Rise of the Creative Class*. Other needs are an active nightlife scene, performing arts spaces, art galleries. Community-oriented development should offer pedestrian-friendly space for these target activities rather than for the expensive array of sports stadiums and convention centers that municipal governments once thought would bolster sagging city centers.

The more talented younger people in Florida's vision of the future will crowd into popular and better-off megaregions such as Boston; San Francisco; Washington, DC; or greater New York City. Within them they would gentrify not just the urban core but outposts such as Jersey City and Hoboken, close to where Florida grew up, the son of a factory worker living in a blue-collar neighborhood in Newark. There is not much space in Florida's "new geography of working and living" to bring back traditional forms of work for residents of the nation's most deprived urban communities—maybe a few service sector jobs. A better bet would be to nurture the creative talent to be found there in, for example, the performing arts. How would he advise the mayor of bereft Camden, New Jersey, I asked him at a conference. "Go find the best music in town," Florida replied.

In Florida's view government is too flimsy a force to "generate the enormous level of demand required for sustained growth." Arts become key components of the new economy's "creative engine" that, linked to technological know-how, generates "all kinds of inventive new goods and services." Paul Hawken, the forward-thinking businessman who cowrote the excellent book *Natural Capitalism*, agrees, finding that no string of governmental interventions has the strength to power the much-needed radical transformations in how we live and what we use that he feels are in progress. The patterns of healing and design that will carry the day, Hawken wrote, "must arise from all levels of society, not just the top." The way government can best assist the transformation is by reducing or eliminating the subsidies that support the old economy—road building and widening, mortgage interest tax deductions—and doing a better job of regulating the very financial institutions that pushed the nation into deep recession in 2008.

—◦—

At the philosophical core of this movement, some of its top thinkers feel, there lies the need for planners and strategists to abandon the mechanistic worldviews of Descartes and Newton and sign on to a new paradigm. Cartesian thought, wrote the physicist Fritjof Capra, is based on the idea that "in every complex system the behavior of the whole can be understood entirely from the properties of its parts." On the contrary, Capra contends, biologists of recent times have built on thought reaching as far back as Aristotle to arrive at exactly the opposite conclusion:

that "the properties of the parts are not intrinsic properties but can be understood only within the context of the larger whole." Aggregation rather than disaggregation lies at the heart of "whole systems analysis," in which the adjective "linear," shorthand for the clumsy way most of us bluntly think about a subject without considering side effects, becomes a pejorative, the opposite of the preferred "holistic."

Ecological and human communities are closely linked by the same principles of organization and can best be understood once this new ecological paradigm becomes recognized and respected. "No individual organism can exist in isolation," writes Capra, a professor at the University of California, Berkeley and founder of its Center for Ecoliteracy and currently a ranking practitioner of nonlinear thinking.

Capra fleshes out his hypothesis by examining disciplines ranging from fractal geometry to quantum physics and Gestalt psychology, starting with a careful examination of the very origins of life on earth. He cites scientists with names not familiar to most of us but who are important for their contributions to the whole-systems idea. "Wherever we see life, we see networks," he writes. And we see dynamic processes, creativity, the generation of new forms "constantly reaching out into novelty." In his analysis of organizational behavior, he suggests ways for leaders to generate dynamic positive feedback loops arranged so that something "good" gets reinforced and becomes better through interaction with something else. "We do not need to invent sustainable human communities from scratch," he argues. We "can model them after nature's ecosystems, which are sustainable communities of plants, animals, and microorganisms."

To whole-systems thinkers, among them the Boston-based architect and planner Bill Reed, the very notion of sustainability—breaking even—is far from adequate. Taking steps to make things get worse at a slower rate is not good enough. Reed aspires to regeneration, leaving a place better after development has taken place. His Integrative Design Collaborative's approach to planning, be it a building or a human settlement, stems from the notion that communities and landscapes are "living organisms" that change continuously. Development can manipulate those forces in constructive, mutually reinforcing ways, contributing to the "health and ongoing vitality of all the natural, cultural, and economic systems that it affects."

In his planning work Reed insists that ideas should not be presented in ways that only experts in computer modeling or systems thinking can comprehend but rather be guided by and emerge from constructive interactions with citizen stakeholders and rendered "into meaningful forms that relate to the average citizen's experience and that inspire and enable them to create a more beneficial relationship with the place they live in." Reed spends much of his time hurtling around the country and the world to participate in intensive whole-systems, multidisciplinary charrettes to guide more detailed thinking about planning and designing structures or communities. He gets more satisfaction from participating in group efforts of this sort than he previously got from designing individual structures.

When we worked closely some years ago, as consultants designing a sustainable-development master plan for biodiverse St. Mary's County in southern Maryland, Reed would often chide me for slipping back into "linear" patterns of thought. In my household, too, I get teased for being "linear" when I try to finish making the salad dressing before starting to grill the fish. But even I, for all the tugs back into Cartesian modes of analysis, have come to appreciate the value of the whole-systems approach and of Reed's idea that regenerative development planning should aim not just to leave a place no worse off than it was but to "actually contribute to the health and ongoing vitality of all the natural, cultural, and economic systems that it affects."

The advanced thoughts of Florida, Capra, Hawken, and Reed all support an intellectual basis for new kinds of community design and organization. So do those of Pavan Sukhdev, a classically trained economist who works for Deutsche Bank and treasures what remains of the planet's precious biodiversity. A group of scholars he gathered has been working under the auspices of the United Nations Environmental Programme in a comprehensive effort, named The Economics of Ecosystems and Biodiversity (TEEB), to show how, if natural capital such as forests or watersheds were valued for the free environmental services they provide, both humans and nature would be far better off. Forests sequester carbon and help the planet cope with global warming, supply endless quantities of foods and fiber, anchor the soil, and help counter erosion and flooding. Coral reefs supply food and medicines and protect shorelines from the full impact of ocean waves. Salt marshes, tidal estuaries such as the Hudson, and mangroves serve as habitat and nursery for many commercially important marine species.

Half a billion people depend on the services provided by coral reefs, which as a consequence of climate change and ocean acidification are in sharp decline. High percentages of the gross domestic product in developing countries like Indonesia, India, and Brazil consist of ecosystem services that, if squandered as they have been, will "perpetuate poverty." TEEB's analysis, constructed on the basis of more than 120 policy action case studies, applies not just to tropical hot spots of biodiversity. A prominent example is the Hudson Valley, whose watershed protection measures enable New York City to bypass the federally mandated requirement for hugely expensive new water treatment facilities if quality standards are not maintained and cost far less. Sukhdev cites a study published in 2007 showing that, while watershed protection increases New Yorkers' water bills by 9 percent, building the ten billion dollar filtration plant would double them.

Sukhdev sees a world in which human and ecosystem health are inextricably intertwined. Yet at the moment, he finds, "we are not measuring either the value of nature's benefits or the costs of their loss." His research seeks to define what he calls the "Net Positive Impact" of the sorts of services provided by forests, reefs, mangroves, tidal estuaries, protected fisheries, and other biodiversity hot spots. This analysis leads him and his colleagues to call for an end to the "economic invisibility of nature" and to build new ways to "use good economics to conserve wild nature." He calls his groundbreaking work "an appeal to each of us, whether a citizen, policy maker, local administrator, investor, entrepreneur, or academic" to "reflect both on the value of nature, and on the nature of value."

As evidence that his thoughts are not just academic hot air, Sukhdev cites the example of Japan's Sumitomo Trust and Banking Company, which in 2010 launched a "biodiversity fund," built on the basis of stocks of "listed companies that engage in biodiversity and sustainable development." The fund—which invests in small- and medium-size as well as large companies—according to the Association for Sustainable and Responsible Development in Asia, reflects "rising interests towards biodiversity in business community."

As I traveled the Hudson Valley in search of material for this book, I found myself often thinking of its culture and leadership in relation to the broad principles outlined above. In many respects, I find, the valley not always intentionally emerges as a clear example of progress toward the restorative, holistic approaches that Florida and Hawken describe and that Sukhdev and the whole-systems thinkers advocate. The valley lacks the big-league cultural attractions and high-speed "urban metabolism" that make New York City a top destination for eight in ten college graduates, according to data gathered at the peak of the recent financial crisis about where they would prefer to launch their careers.

The Hudson cannot offer young people the technological depth of Boston's Route 128 or Northern California's Silicon Valley or the entertainment allure of a Los Angeles. These too are areas that rank high on young adults' destination scorecards. But yet . . . but yet, the forces at work in the valley closely if quietly resemble those that Florida highlights. Just as he can sense the demise of the "old suburban way of life," in many corners of the Hudson, I find evidence of new creative forces that are distinctively reshaping this region.

Beacon is a prime example. The demise of the Sterling Forest development project, and its antecedent at Storm King Mountain, suggests the power of the ecological values that many of the valley's citizens have come to cherish. Dia:Beacon and the Storm King Art Center speak loudly of how culture thrives in cleaned-up environments and how their ascendancy leads to impacts on the bottom line. Garrison shows how a community can have growth without sprawl. Glynwood and the Rainbeau Ridge farm lead a spirited chorus of believers in healthy food locally grown on small family farms; the movement is especially vigorous in Westchester and Dutchess Counties and in the town of Warwick near Sterling Forest.

Bard College has come out of nowhere to rank among Dutchess County's top employers, and the State University of New York at New Paltz is the number-three employer in Ulster County, with a work force of 3,331 people in the region and a $67.5 million payroll. Student spending there tops $100 million a year. Interim president Donald Christian calls the college "an economic anchor that is a source of stability . . . through all sorts of economic travails."

An apple- and grape-growing farm town of six thousand that is only a two-hour drive from New York City, New Paltz emphasizes a mix of historical and outdoor values. Promotional websites stress the town's rich history as a Huguenot settlement dating to 1677 and its abundance of recreational opportunities. Activities featured on its website include skydiving, horseback riding, rock climbing, yoga at the library, and hiking on the Wallkill Valley Rail Trail. "Bike and Walk whenever possible," exhorts one community site.

Some of what's happening locally reflects broader changes in the marketplace that mesh tightly with Richard Florida's vision. In 1992, 7 percent of all new housing starts in the region were in New York City and over 70 percent were in the urban fringe. Today, more than 70 percent are in the city and less than 20 percent outside. "So what happened?" asks prominent developer Jonathan Rose. "The market changed—bright young people and empty nester older people all want to live in vital, dense communities with great educational, employment (for the younger people) and health care options (for the older population). So now there is an oversupply of suburban housing." And so, Rose and Florida both suggest, there is also rising interest in places like the old, now-reviving Hudson towns that feature not gated suburban golf course communities (from which there is an exodus in some places) but walkable, mixed-use village centers.

"High Tech on the Hudson," headlined the New York *Daily News* over a 2010 story describing the "growing numbers of New Yorkers involved in digital media who are gravitating to Kingston, population 22,441, for the industrial and artsy flavor of Brooklyn combined with the real estate values of the boonies." One such is digital services provider Mark Greene, who moved up from Brooklyn in 2003, joining some five hundred others who had found their way to what he entitled the Kingston Digital Corridor. Said Greene: "The idea was to create an economy of microbusinesses with a diverse client base from outside the area. So there never could be a repeat of the IBM disaster of 1995, when Kingston's main employer ditched the city, leaving behind a 2.4-million-square-foot ghost town." Now, said city official March

Gallagher, "there are a ton of digital professionals in the area. They're bringing New York City money here." A nonprofit incubator deals with filmmakers working in the area. A digital training company has taken root. The former IBM plant has become Tech City, with facilities for renewable energy companies.

Along with this influx has come a rise in interest in redeveloping historical parts of the town, including especially its waterfront along the banks of Rondout Creek, in ways that conform to these newly arrived sophisticates' preferences and aspirations. In 2003 Brooklyn-based real estate entrepreneur Robert Iannucci and his wife Sonia Ewers accepted what turned out to be a fateful invitation to cruise the Hudson aboard the privately owned fireboat *John J. Harvey*. "His motorcycling buddy was the boat's engineer," wrote Betsy Frawley Haggerty in *Northeast Boating Magazine*. "Iannucci, who collects and races vintage motorcycles, expected to spend a couple of days aboard tinkering with the boat's five 45-year-old diesels. Instead, the former Sea Scout fell passionately in love with boating, the Hudson River, and, most significantly, the city of Kingston."

Just three years after he made this discovery, the cigar-chomping Iannucci had bought up thirty-eight parcels representing most of the town's available waterfront land, including almost two miles of its shoreline. He cleared away old junkyards and tank farms. He bought and restored an abandoned navy PT boat of World War II vintage and other historical vessels. He developed close links with the Hudson River Maritime Museum. He wants to launch a tugboat- and industry-oriented museum at another property he owns, the century-old Cornell Steamboat Company Building, to house for restoration some of the debris he found along the shore. He bought an old building called the Ulster Academy and remodeled it into handsome condos with great views.

"My work here is almost done," says this self-styled "dream weaver." But, he quickly adds, he has a major rezoning project on the drawing boards. "I'm not a developer," he says. "I need a partner for that." To date, says former New York State planner Steve Resler, who spent years working on Kingston waterfront issues, Iannucci has repeatedly been "very sensitive" to development limits set in a Local Waterfront Revitalization Plan approved by state and local officials in 1992. When ideas surfaced about major new waterfront projects, Resler continued, Iannucci would urge caution. "Take it easy," he'd say. "Remember, there's a plan in place. You'd better go talk with them."

Separately, the far more conventional commercial company called AVR Realty is moving forward with the major 1,658-unit mixed-use Hudson Landing development on another 535-acre Kingston shorefront site, a former quarry and brickyard that had long ago become a ruin. After six years of sometimes angry jousting about the development's massive size with the Friends of the Kingston Waterfront, a pint-size coalition of environmental groups including Scenic Hudson, AVR modified its plan. The original version, said *Hudson Valley* magazine, "would have created massive suburban sprawl" along the shoreline. Later, responding to the pressures, the company scaled back the number of housing units to be built and incorporated many "new urbanist" neo-traditional neighborhood design features into the final package. Accused of having disregarded the town's Local Waterfront Revitalization Plan, the company reduced Hudson Landing's dimensions down from a massive 2,200 units for the sake of preserving viewsheds and open space and responded to environmentalists' concerns about sewage, transportation, and biodiversity issues. "You know what?" said one Kingston alderman. "The developer gave a lot."

As of late 2010 the project had received all required clearances, and the company was breaking ground for its Phase I. City officials expressed delight about increases in the local tax base and about the project's representing a "shot in the arm," as Kingston economic and community development director Stephen Finkle put it in a newspaper interview, for a stagnant place badly in need of one in the wake of the IBM pullout. The company, Scenic Hudson's Jeffrey Anzevino, and Kingston's mayor Jim Sottile have all said that the project is now far better designed thanks to the exhausting environmental review process. "As originally proposed it was a strung out mass of sprawl," says Anzevino. "It's not perfect now, but it is substantially improved, worlds above what was first proposed, with village-like arrangements of buildings and moving them off of the most prominent ridge lines."

Respectful of Richard Florida's scenarios, Hudson Landing is being reconfigured to appeal to singles and empty nesters fleeing suburbs and in search of a new lifestyle. While some environmentalists are still grumbling about the project's magnitude and remain aloof, Rob Iannucci welcomes his new neighbor: "Anything that makes the city grow is good for me," he says. "They need me more than I need them. We create reasons for people to come to Kingston." Broadly, he sees blue skies ahead for a reason having to do with boating, not the digital invasion: because of Kingston's strategic location as the only harbor on the Hudson north of New York City. "The Hub of the Hudson Valley" this energetically creative leader called this long-neglected place as, after our brief introduction on the phone, he proposed that I buy one of his Ulster Academy condos.

Even in the new century, where thinking around Kingston among planners and developers has come a long way from what it was back in the 1980s, conflicts do not always get resolved as smoothly as they were at Hudson Landing. Another proposed development project called Sailor's Cove consists of 360 units on eighty strategically located acres. Sponsors presented the planning board with a design that the *Kingston Times* called "hopelessly stuck in the 1980s" and "a wretched mass of swinger-apartment-style cul-de-sacs." Despite opposition from many quarters, reports Scenic Hudson's Anzevino, the developers continued to "thumb their noses at the planning board" and ended up suing the city. You can't win 'em all. But for all the pitfalls along the way, Anzevino says, you can add Kingston to the lengthening roster of Hudson Valley communities struggling with considerable success to adapt to citizens' changing values and priorities.

Take even the worst case, that of the port of Newburgh just north of Storm King Mountain. Designated by *Look* magazine as an "All-American City" back in 1952, this city of almost thirty thousand held on for a while during the mid-twentieth century, living off the fat of a rich commercial and industrial heritage. Then Newburgh floundered. A federally funded 1970s urban renewal effort failed: Many houses were destroyed, none built. Newburgh has a dysfunctional political system in which the offices of mayor and city manager both come equipped with revolving doors. Farther afield, decay gives way to sprawl. Yawning Stewart Field, with long runways and light air traffic, is a perennial candidate to become New York's fourth jetport. But for the moment this former air force base is little used by the airlines or anybody else, and in recent years even that usage has dwindled. The hitch, not likely to be solved anytime soon: the lack of direct train service to New York City.

Today this factory town without many factories has a severely depressed downtown where deep poverty persists: The 2000 census found 23 percent of the population living below the poverty line. Newburgh has a violent crime rate 739 percent greater than the average for New York State and 406 percent greater than the national average. "Welcome to Newburgh, murder capital of New York State," blared *New York* magazine in an extensive fall 2011 piece about the town's long history of gang culture. Drug traffic remains blatant along side streets leading off Broadway, the town's wide, empty main drag.

One blazing-hot summer afternoon, I crept by car along downtown Newburgh's forlorn side streets in the manner of an anxious drug buyer, ready to hit the accelerator hard, as I looked for sculptor Stuart Sachs's unnumbered loft building. Few pedestrians; a scattering of cars parked on the shabby, treeless streets; people sitting on stoops. A sense of tension and hostility. Then there magically appeared, out of a small community service building, a stunningly beautiful midteens girl with glowing brown skin and smoldering eyes. She knew exactly where Sachs was and pointed me toward the hidden doorway.

So how to help fashion a better life for that glistening kid? The odds are long, but surprisingly, even this problem-ridden place has a notable recent history of involvement in restorative activities, in reclaiming a battered urban environment and gaining hard-won ground against political and social disarray. Waterfront revitalization has begun to happen here as well as in better-off communities, in an area adjacent to the terminal of the ferry that crosses the river to Beacon. A new restaurant there has replaced a nightclub with a bad reputation.

In 2009 Ray Yannone, a lifelong Newburgher, bought the city's roofless, long-abandoned West Shore railroad station with trees growing inside, the only building on Water Street that survived the botched urban renewal blitz. The structure had for many years, said *Valley Table* magazine, "sat like a carcass on the side of the road." Yannone got financing from local banks, renovated the building, and turned it into a nonprofit performing arts center (listen up, Richard Florida) with several tenants and a new cafe. Early in 2011, despite a stormy winter, all available space was rented out.

The new Orange County Community College building called the Newburgh Extension Center sharply punctuates lower Broadway's seedy cityscape. The college has embarked on a one hundred million dollar expansion named the Newburgh Branch Campus. Ten million dollars of the funding has been supplied by the tireless business leader William Kaplan, who has also supported student scholarships and countless educational programs and regularly hectors Albany in search of state and federal funds for his hard-pressed hometown. His foundation has also invested ten million dollars toward a downtown expansion of the local hospital and supported the renovation of a badly run-down National Guard armory building near Broadway into a business, sports, and arts and crafts activities center.

Historic Liberty Street, running parallel to the river and largely boarded up not long ago, has attracted new businesses. The Newburgh Preservation Association works to increase awareness of the town's four thousand historical houses. Another group strives to restore a rare, four-hundred-year-old Dutch Reformed Church sitting high on a hillside. Within the ghetto, sculptor and furniture builder Stuart Sachs found that hidden building I had trouble locating. First used in about 1870 as a stable and later a plumbing supply shop, it had become a shooting gallery for drug addicts. Sachs filled up five forty-yard Dumpsters of trash and during the hot summer of 2010 was cheerfully making the vast interior space into a studio for him and a rental loft for income. When he goes home, he locks three doors behind him.

The dapper, talented Luke Ives Pontifell operates his business, Thornwillow Press, in another old loft building in the heart of the ghetto. He employs dedicated local people, many of them Latinos, who use rare old handpresses and binding equipment to make fine-quality books on handmade paper and leather-bind them. Pontifell lives in New York City and commutes to work via the Metro-North train to Beacon and then takes the trans-Hudson ferry.

Habitat for Humanity, the ecumenical religious organization that recruits volunteers to build or restore housing for the poor, has been working in east Newburgh since 1999 and has compiled a commendable record of accomplishment. As of late 2010 it had built or restored a total of forty-three houses in what had been a totally abandoned part of town; 225 people, some of whom had served as construction workers on the project, had occupied these dwellings. For Newburgh, Habitat for Humanity's efforts had as of mid-2011 resulted in a twelve million dollar increase in assessed property values. The appearance of bright new homes in formerly abandoned parts of town, wrote Habitat for Humanity staff member Shala Carlson on the organization's website, sparks a "sense of renewal, an undeniable feeling that—with enough financial and moral support—Newburgh can revitalize." One example of the spirit the organization arouses: In April 2011 the twelfth annual Walk for Housing event attracted six hundred walkers who raised forty thousand dollars.

Another current effort is focused on saving and restoring the old brick Ritz Theater. Located strategically on the main drag, this structure dates back to 1883 and in 1913 became a performing arts center named Cohen's Opera House. Later renamed the Ritz, the theater achieved notable moments. It was the birthplace of actress Lucille Ball's *I Love Lucy* show and the site of young Frank Sinatra's stage debut, singing with the Tommy Dorsey orchestra to a surprised and delighted audience. Shows en route to Broadway tried out there, as they did in New Haven.

But decline set in during the 1960s. The Ritz, its stage walled off in 1969, limped along as a movie house until 1981, when, after vandalism, it shut down completely. Restoration efforts began in 2002, when a nonprofit group called Safe Harbors of the Hudson, concerned with housing and the arts, bought the structure and turned its lobby into a 125-seat theater. Now planned is a proud new 825-seat theater that, once the renovation is completed, will offer a brighter future, when Newburgh's last remaining historical theater will once again be able to offer live performances. Previously, Safe Harbors had already won its stripes by buying the old Hotel Newburgh, adjacent to the Ritz on Main Street, which had become a run-down welfare hotel. Now called the Cornerstone Residence, the renovated building is split into 116 "supportive housing" units for single adults with special needs and 12 lofts for artists.

In 2006 a weeklong charrette was held to discuss planning for the city, especially its mile-long waterfront and an adjacent thirty acres of vacant land. The intensive planning exercise, which attracted six hundred people, was conducted by new urbanist icon Andres Duany of the well-known Miami-based Duany Plater-Zyberk firm, under a public-private partnership arrangement. Partners include his firm, the city of Newburgh, and a master developer, Leyland Alliance, that specializes in traditional neighborhood designs. Thanks to the Great Recession's housing market conditions, not much has yet been done to implement the resulting design. When and if it happens, wrote Duany, the work will be "guided by the old-fashioned notion that the most successful cities include neighborhoods for all kinds of people, accessible retail areas, walkable streets, and wonderful parks and public spaces."

Many of the principles that emerged from the charrette survive in an inch-thick Sustainable Master Plan, to which many committed citizens also contributed time and effort, that says all the right things about how to make the place "a thriving, walkable and attractive community." In 2008 Plan-It Newburgh was approved by the city council, and piecemeal implementation slowly continues. It supersedes all previous plans for the city. Land use regulations now being worked on must by law conform to it.

Howard Kaufman, a Leyland Alliance executive, says his company is keen to get started on implementing the Duany design and launching other projects along the Newburgh waterfront. He admits that times were still tough in 2011, with an administratively weak municipal government fixated on economic survival and without funds to build the infrastructure that is required before privately financed development could begin. With funding of any sort in critically short supply, Kaufman admitted that Leyland was so far taking no more than "baby steps" on a single block near Broadway, where the company has built three houses as part of the Habitat for Humanity program, toward more comprehensive participation in Newburgh's revival. But he has no doubt that Newburgh's renaissance will soon take off, with a "great spirit" afoot, and new "anchors" in view.

Ray Yannone agrees. Heavy property taxes remain a problem, he says. Still, he says, "this is an opportune moment here. A lot of positive things are coming together at the same time." Suggesting the possibility that Newburgh has bottomed out, *New York* magazine noted in its October 2011 article, "No one in Newburgh will tell you so without immediately touching wood, but so far this year, there has not been a single gang-related homicide."

Bill Kaplan, who seems consistently capable of pulling rabbits out of hats, expresses special pride in what was done in 2010, in a quick burst of intensive activity, to revive the old armory building. He supplied a grant of one hundred thousand dollars to Habitat for Humanity, which fielded a volunteer labor force to refurbish the building's basketball floor and install bathrooms and other facilities for the handicapped. A nonprofit was founded to attract recreational, educational, and corporate tenants for parts of the building and to recruit both the community college and the private Mount Saint Mary College as partners and users of the facility. Kaplan professes only a modest role in making it happen. "Everything fit together," he says. "There was a great need and a great opportunity. Now the trick is to make it self-sustaining."

Others say it could never have happened without Kaplan in the mix. Said the *Mid Hudson Times:* "If anyone was wondering how the City of Newburgh was going to pull off the resurrection of the old Armory, they needed only to look at Bill Kaplan, a man of miracles. . . . When he takes on a project, he doesn't hold back." Now, without success so far, he is trying to find tenants for the partly renovated Regal Bag building, a long-dormant 160-year-old cotton mill on the waterfront where he himself works. This is one of many problems that he faces, but his resolve remains firm. "Don't make me sound negative," he warns.

———

In 2009 the high-rolling Broadway impresario Rocco Landesman became chairman of the National Endowment for the Arts, an unlikely but appealing choice. Soon after settling in, he began looking for ways to tilt the small but influential institution's windmill. Eventually, he and Ford Foundation president Luis Ubiñas came up with an idea for a program that would play in Newburgh—by putting the arts in the forefront of economic development. Called ArtPlace, says NEA's handout, the program offers "a new model of helping towns and cities thrive, by strategically integrating artists and arts organizations into key local efforts in transportation, housing, community development, job creation, and more."

ArtPlace, NEA continues, "neither treats the arts as an add-on nor expects development to follow on its own from stand-alone investments in cultural projects." Rather, its cultural grants occur in holistic "concert with other community partners, private and public." Landesman called them "vital drivers of community revitalization and development."

"It's all about connecting things in places where momentum is already occurring," says ArtPlace president Carol Coletta.

In late summer 2011 ArtPlace announced its first round of winners, thirty-four locally initiated projects across the nation that would receive a total of $11.5 million in grants from a consortium of foundations. In several instances the grants support arts projects also involving reuse of old buildings, transportation initiatives, or other forms of "creative placemaking." In Detroit's faded downtown, for example, ArtPlace made a cluster of grants to help create the Sugar Hill Arts District along an abandoned stretch of once-elegant Woodward Avenue. The ArtPlace money comes not from the foundations' own coffers but in the form of loans from six major financial institutions. Federal agencies participate not as funders, but as nonvoting partners whose participation is intended to encourage symmetry between ArtPlace grants and federal policies and programs. Ubiñas, chair of the ArtPlace President's Council, called it a "new paradigm" for its "integrated, interwoven approach."

And indeed, a range of big thinkers were applauding. "By God they got it!" exclaimed the urban critic Roberta Brandes Gratz. "They finally got it!" She praises the ArtPlace consortium for its "pledge to invest generously in locally-formed, modest scale cultural enterprises as generators of urban rebirth." She labels the town of Hudson, showing multiple small steps of regeneration that "eventually add up to big change," as a choice site for ArtPlace attention.

Another is Newburgh, with its surprising cluster of energetic cultural initiatives already well under way. College student Alyssa Alfano, a Newburgh native, recently discovered a whole new world out there. "Although my father and his parents were born and raised in the city," she wrote in the OurHudson blog,

> *I rarely found myself in downtown Newburgh during my childhood . . . we had no reason to go: there were few restaurants that we frequented and hardly any entertainment or activities. . . . During my senior year of high school, I heard about a café that had opened in*

the city, but I hardly considered it and continued to foster my teenage caffeine addiction at a Starbucks in the more affluent Town of Newburgh. On a whim, two friends and I (bored of the typical suburban mall hangout) decided to venture to this new café. We were incredibly surprised by its sidewalk seating, well decorated interior, eclectic menu, and most importantly, location. In an area we thought we would have never otherwise set foot in, we found ourselves enjoying hibiscus iced teas and paninis.

Here's to you, Alyssa. May you find a niche somewhere in Richard Florida's universe that will move you to join the grand national reset of which he writes and speaks. And here's to you all, the many citizens whose innovations and enthusiasms I describe on these pages, for what you have already done to revive, brand, enliven, and enrich a very special and compelling place that is well along in resetting itself. This book will doubtless be accused of not having paid adequate attention either to ongoing environmental degradation or to human suffering in the region. I freely admit these shortcomings. But those stories belong in some other place. The most powerful emotion I found along the Hudson was hope.

Acknowledgments

WHEN YOU LAY THEM ALL END TO END, THE NEW FORCES FAVORING environmentally sound change in the Hudson Valley have become very powerful, I contend, and the outlook for the longer term is positive, despite the heavy economic storm clouds that currently blacken the skies. The chapter notes that follow name some of the many publications that are prominently cited in the text. Dozens of people referred to there guided me regarding specifics. Here I list those who, in a more general sense, helped make this book happen.

While living in New York City during the 1970s, I began spending weekends with my wife and daughter and dog in Cornwall-on-Hudson near West Point. While there, I was well exposed to the environmental issues that had surfaced during those times. Constantine and Anne Sidamon-Eristoff, wise tutors, gave sound thoughts and warm and generous hospitality. Neighbors and treasured friends Steve and Smokey Duggan and Esty and Hellie Stowell, all now deceased, were stalwart leaders in the environmental battles of those years, and masterful guides. Also most helpful were the thoughts of the Natural Resources Defense Council's founder John Adams, based just across the river in Garrison, and his influential neighbors Fred Rich and Fred Osborn III. David Redden, another Cornwall neighbor, kindly arranged for me to join him on Scenic Hudson's board. I stayed for several years and learned a lot. Pete Seeger, whom I had interviewed in 1961 while working as a *Time* magazine correspondent, was of course an inspiration for his passion about the Hudson and its health.

Much later, having thought and written extensively about the relationship between economics and the environment in far-flung coastal and tropical forest areas, I turned my attention to places closer to home. In 2008 I fastened on the Hudson Valley as a leading example of a region's recovery from a grimy industrial past and drafted a book outline. "This has to happen," said dear friend Elizabeth ("Symmie") Newhouse, for many years a senior editor at *National Geographic.* She generously helped improve the proposal and had me pass it along to the talented agent Carol Mann. Carol in turn generated interest on the part of Janice Goldklang at Globe Pequot Press, a gifted editor with whom I had worked many years before, and the book was under way.

Bob Anderberg of the Open Space Institute, Ned Sullivan of Scenic Hudson, and Ashton Hawkins were chief among the many who took precious time to show me around. From the privileged vantage point of a golf cart, I saw the wonderful Storm King Art Center through the keen eyes of its gifted longtime president, Peter Stern, and stalwart director and curator David Collens. Stewart and Sarah Kagan and their daughter spent a long and pleasant Sunday introducing me to the family farming revolution in Westchester County. No one beat the drums for my project more energetically than the veteran Hudson Valley steward Barnabas McHenry. Wint Aldrich gave me large increments of his time to discuss the valley's abundance of historical houses and guide me toward troves of information.

Along the course of my travels up and down the valley, Herschel and Peggy Post, George Muser, Douglas and Sarah Banker, and the Stowells' sons and daughters—Frank, Esty Jr., Jenipher, and Lally—kindly provided lodgings. Furthermore, the publishing grants program of the J.M. Kaplan Fund extended two much-needed increments of financial support. So did my old friend William L. Bernhard. My deep thanks go to these most welcome donors. The New York State Library in Albany; the New York Historical Society; and libraries at Marist College, the Stowell family residence, and Cornwall, New York, yielded useful nuggets of information that Google, for all its power, had yet to find.

My deep thanks to all the above.

My wife, Flo, to whom this work is dedicated, believed fervently in the project from the start and never let me lose heart. I cherish her wonderfully moving spirit and enthusiasm.

Chapter Notes

For general information on the Hudson's past and present, I should especially note one film project: Bill Moyers's two-hour miniseries *America's First River*, which aired on PBS in 2002. As of this writing filmmaker Jasper Goldman was still putting together *Hudson Rising*, a twenty-eight-minute film stressing this book's themes that was scheduled for PBS airing early in 2012 and will become a valuable resource.

The 2010 documentary *Gasland* by Josh Fox, a surprise award winner at the 2010 Sundance Film Festival, remains the principal film about the consequences of environmentally risky "fracking," the colloquial name for the method of drilling for natural gas that threatens the Catskills and New York City's water supply.

What follows is a chapter-by-chapter listing of the principal print sources on which I drew.

Chapter 1

The battle to stop St. Lawrence Cement from further defacement of the shorefront at and near the town of Hudson is fully described in Miriam D. Silverman's *Stopping the Plant: The St. Lawrence Cement Controversy and the Battle for Quality of Life in the Hudson Valley* (State University of New York Press 2006). The final chapter of Tom Lewis's *The Hudson: A History* (Yale University Press 2005) offers a tidy summary of the principal twentieth-century issues in the valley.

Chapter 2

For insight into the passions of Hudson River School artists and the writers who shared their views, there is much to learn from the art historian Barbara Babcock Lassiter's book *American Wilderness: The Hudson River School of Painting* (Doubleday 1978), from Frances E. Dunwell's handsome volume *The Hudson: America's River* (Columbia University Press 2008), and from Raymond J. O'Brien's *American Sublime: Landscape and Scenery of the Lower Hudson Valley* (Columbia University Press 1981). The many writings of Nathaniel Parker Willis, especially his *Outdoors at Idlewild* (Scribner 1855) offered inspiration, as did Carl Carmer's classic *The Hudson* (Holt, Rinehart & Winston 1939). Lewis Beach's most often cited enthusiasm for the village of Cornwall is in his book *Cornwall* (E. M. Ruttenber & Son 1873). Edith Wharton's *Hudson River Bracketed* (D. Appleton & Co. 1929) provided amusement. Dr. Edward Partridge most clearly enunciated his proposal that the Hudson Valley achieve national park status in his November 1907 article in *Outlook* magazine. Robert O. Binnewies's *Palisades: 100,000 Acres in 100 Years* (Fordham University Press 2001), while short on detail about the important role of land-protection organizations such as the Open Space Institute, does knowledgeably summarize the political and philanthropic dynamics of how a major interstate park evolved in New York and New Jersey, in the very shadow of the giant metropolis.

Chapter 3

As noted in the main text, the classic book about the Con Edison fracas at Storm King Mountain is Allan R. Talbot's *Power along the Hudson* (E. P. Dutton 1972). Robert Boyle's sharp-tongued *The Hudson: A Natural and Unnatural History*, first published in 1969 by W. W. Norton and expanded and updated a decade later, was powerful tonic at its time and remains a benchmark description of the estuary's ecology. John and Patricia Adams's *A Force for Nature: The Story of NRDC and the Fight to Save Our Planet* (Chronicle Books 2010) adds perspective to the authors' thoughts about the Storm King events. So does *The Riverkeepers* by John Cronin and Robert F. Kennedy Jr. (Simon & Schuster 1997). Exhaustive coverage of the complex role in the valley of the Rockefeller family can be found in *The Rockefellers: An American Dynasty* by Peter Collier and David Horowitz (Holt, Rinehart & Winston 1976). As for DeWitt and Lila Wallace, John Heidenry's *Theirs Was the Kingdom* (Norton 1993) and Peter Canning's *American Dreamers* (Simon & Schuster 1996) both examine in vivid detail the decline and fall of the imperious *Reader's Digest* family and how a solid chunk of the fortune they had amassed fell into the hands of land conservationists.

Chapter 4

Neil Maher's description of Black Rock Forest appears in his article, "A Very Pleasant Place to Build a Towne On," published in 1999 in the excellent *Hudson Valley Regional Review* by the Hudson River Valley Institute at Marist College. See also "The Story of Black Rock," by Nicole A. Buzzetto-More in the Spring 2006 issue of the *Hudson River Valley Review*. The book *Saving Sterling Forest*, by the late activist Ann Botshon (State University of New York Press 2007), gives you an insider's blow-by-blow account of a remarkable achievement.

Chapter 5

Essential reading on the big subject of New York City's supply of clean freshwater begins with Gerard T. Koeppel's *Water for Gotham: A History* (Princeton University Press 2000). Another rich lode of information is in *Liquid Assets: A History of New York City's Water System*

(Purple Mountain Press 1999) by Diane Galusha, a former journalist now working on water issues for New York City and an interviewee in this book. Stunning coverage of the elegant system's design falls within the covers of *Water-Works, The Architecture and Engineering of the New York City Water Supply* (Kevin Bone, Ed.; Monacelli Press 2006). Though the media coverage of natural gas drilling in the Marcellus Shale has been extensive, as of fall 2011 I know of no full-length book on the subject. The *New York Times* published an arresting series by Ian Urbina.

Chapter 6
Planner Peter Manning expresses his reverence for the Hudson Valley landscape in his article, "Developing the Middle Landscape: The Shawangunk Carriage Roads," in the Autumn 2010 issue of the *Hudson River Valley Review*. Heavily cited both in this book and in Governor Andrew Cuomo's campaign literature is environmental historian David Stradling's *The Nature of New York: An Environmental History of the Empire State* (Cornell University Press 2010). At the head of a small bookshelf of literature by or about the designer Russel Wright is Robert Schonfeld's *Russel Wright: Creating American Lifestyle* (Smithsonian Institution 2002).

Chapter 7
A loving account of the fall and rise of Denning's Point in Beacon, replete with interesting archival photos, is Jim Heron's *Denning's Point: A Hudson River History* (Black Dome Press 2006).

Chapter 8
The Open Space Institute, the American Farmland Trust, and the Glynwood Center all supply copious information about how to do

sustainable agriculture. *Over the Rainbeau* (Rainbeau Ridge Publishing 2009), by Lisa Schwartz, Judith Hausman, and Karen Sabath, describes the team's advance from suburban comforts toward the passions and headaches of local and sustainable farming. Also in the book are some great recipes.

Chapter 9

Not for the fainthearted reader is a climbing guide to the fabled cliffs of the Shawangunks entitled *The Climber's Guide to the Shawangunks* (Vulgarian Press 2001), by Dick Williams. He gives you a general picture of the area and also details down to the last toehold, in prose unfathomable for the lay reader, your best routes upward.

Chapter 10

The *New York Times* covered the controversy over the Westway road-building project in something like a thousand separate stories, and media attention remained keen as the plans for the Hudson River Park took shape. For general background on the ideologies and forces in play, see Jane Jacobs's classic *The Death and Life of Great American Cities* (Random House 1961) and her subsequent *The Economy of Cities* (Random House 1969). Despite its great heft, another must-read is *The Power Broker* (Knopf 1974), Anthony Caro's Pulitzer Prize-winning biography of planner Robert Moses. The Hudson River Park website offers a rich trove of information about how the plan evolved and what's cooking there now. The improbable tale of how the High Line came to be is captured in vivid detail in *High Line: The Inside Story of New York City's Park in the Sky,* by Joshua David and Robert Hammond (Farrar, Straus and Giroux 2011). The authors, neither of whom had any prior experience either with landscape design or with tackling the hydra-headed New York City bureaucracy, led the miraculously successful, decade-long effort to save the High Line from demolition and create a park that has profoundly transformed New York City's West Side.

Chapter 11

As of this writing, no book-length summary of the ground covered by the Quadricentennial Commission has yet surfaced. Stay tuned via visits to the OurHudson website, which as 2011 ended was remaining active. Likewise, though media coverage of the Marcellus Shale fracking issues has been intense, we still have no book-length coverage of the subject as it applies to New York.

Chapter 12

The classic work by urbanist Richard Florida is *The Rise of the Creative Class* (Basic Books 2002). His more recent *The Great Reset: How New Ways of Living and Working Drive Post-Crash Prosperity* (HarperCollins 2010) more directly relates to my major themes. So does *Natural Capitalism: Creating the Next Industrial Revolution* (Little, Brown 1997), the highly influential book that business leader Paul Hawken coauthored with Hunter and Amory Lovins. Of several books by physicist Fritjof Capra, the one I would especially note is *The Web of Life: A New Scientific Understanding of Living Systems* (Anchor Books 1996). Pavan Sukhdev's ideas are well summarized in a booklet entitled "The Economics of Ecosystems and Biodiversity: Mainstreaming the Economics of Nature: A synthesis of the approach, conclusions, and recommendations of TEEB," published in 2010 by the United Nations Environmental Programme.

Index

255